ADVANCE PRAISE FOR

American Public Education Law Primer

"David C. Bloomfield has written a user-friendly guide to education law that will prove extremely helpful to parents, teachers, and all others concerned about public education."

Diane Ravitch, Research Professor, Steinhardt School of Culture, Education, and Human Development, New York University

American Public Education Law

PRIMER

PETER LANG
New York • Washington, D.C./Baltimore • Bern
Frankfurt am Main • Berlin • Brussels • Vienna • Oxford

David C. Bloomfield

American Public Education Law

PRIMER

PETER LANG
New York • Washington, D.C./Baltimore • Bern
Frankfurt am Main • Berlin • Brussels • Vienna • Oxford

Library of Congress Cataloging-in-Publication Data

Bloomfield, David C.
American public education law primer / David C. Bloomfield.
p. cm. — (Peter Lang primers)
Includes bibliographical references.
1. Educational law and legislation—United States. I. Title.
KF4119.8.E3B56 344.73'071—dc22 2007003073
ISBN 978-1-4331-0038-3 (hardcover)
ISBN 978-0-8204-7948-4 (paperback)

Bibliographic information published by **Die Deutsche Bibliothek**.
Die Deutsche Bibliothek lists this publication in the "Deutsche Nationalbibliografie"; detailed bibliographic data is available on the Internet at http://dnb.ddb.de/.

Cover design by Clear Point Designs

The paper in this book meets the guidelines for permanence and durability of the Committee on Production Guidelines for Book Longevity of the Council of Library Resources.

29 Broadway, 18th floor, New York, NY 10006
www.peterlang.com

Printed in the United States of America

Contents

Foreword

This unique book provides an introduction to American public education law for college and graduate students, educators, and parents. Rather than merely rehashing the canon of Supreme Court case law on public education, the book draws on typical fact patterns that everyone in the field will recognize: teacher firings; curriculum decisions; student dress and discipline; inequitable treatment based on race, sex, or handicapping condition; child abuse; school board conduct; and more. Analysis of these facts through various local, state, and federal legal sources—constitutional, statutory, regulatory, and judicial—yields a comprehensive, practical introduction to American education law that is both understandable and sophisticated. This is how lawyers really work and how the wise educator or parent can best become legally informed and active.

The first chapter presents the innovative "Cascade of American Education Law". This helpful metaphor elegantly frames our myriad sources of law within a single concept. American law cascades from the

Constitution, downward to state and federal legislative enactments, to regulations, to the regulatory guidance that drives so many real-world decisions. Each level requires consistency with provisions "upriver," giving coherence to a legal system that often seems fractured and chaotic. The courts, with their own cascade of powers, largely interpret laws created by the other branches of government. The interplay of these forces ("the Cascade Game") has profound implications for practitioners who want to control their legal destinies. Finally, the chapter provides a helpful tutorial on basic legal research. This skill, so basic to a robust democracy, provides the book's lay audience with access to material, detailed in the Resources and References, usually known only to legal professionals.

Chapter 2 addresses, primarily, issues involving student rights: expression, discipline, and church/state separation. But in a wide-ranging discussion of these topics, the roles of legislation and political advocacy are also explored, making this chapter a mini-handbook for those who seek to change the law, as well as follow it. Everyone knows the frustrations of obeying laws that seem frivolous, cumbersome, or simply wrong. But the attitude that "you can't fight city hall" breeds a demoralizing sense of resignation among professionals and the public that debilitates our public schools. If we use the lessons taught here—that the law is a dynamic, changeable set of rules subject to organized citizen action—then we become masters of our legal fate, not mere objects of arbitrary, static decisions. It is striking that many of the fact situations treated in this chapter turn on application of school and district policies rather than major legislative or judicial pronouncements. By aiming low at these powerful local sources of law, many legal battles can be won without bringing out the heavy artillery of expensive lobbyists or high-powered lawyers.

Chapter 3 broadens the horizon from individual students and schools to issues primarily affecting school districts. What are the parameters of curricular decision making and of selecting controversial materials for school libraries? When might educator actions on field trips or child abuse reporting result in termination or even criminal charges? What exposure might a district suffer if school reform efforts exclude certain groups of disabled or "limited English proficient" students? These are the kinds of questions district administrators routinely face but that are rarely addressed in introductory education law texts. Dealing with these practical legal problems requires dexterity and facility with complex contemporary legal arrangements, skills cultivated in the chapter's attention to the role of administrative agencies in modern American education law.

Nowhere has this shifting legal landscape been more apparent than in the role of state and federal governments in micro-managing contemporary public education. Once, principals and superintendents ruled their roosts, paying scant attention to governmental units beyond the district, save perhaps to calculate additional funding streams. Now, as we all know, the full regulatory apparatus of governmental oversight has been visited upon public schools, along with increasing judicial scrutiny. Chapter 4 describes the dimensions of state and federal involvement in special education, testing, and student records, which often dominate the news and require so much time from those of us toiling in the vineyards of public education.

In many ways, this book is a call to action by someone who has lived the many facets of American education law. Currently a professor and head of the graduate educational leadership program at Brooklyn College, CUNY, the author has a notable record as an elementary and middle school teacher, parent leader, government official, and lawyer in private and school district practice. An honors graduate of Columbia University School of Law with a graduate degree in public affairs from Princeton, he has drafted legislation, litigated, negotiated, lobbied, organized, and counseled. Though grounded in scholarship, this book is a product of his extensive field experience as an educator, activist, and attorney.

However much we can learn here, the knowledge gained will be squandered if it is not acted upon. And such action is unavoidable, because we do not live in a legal vacuum. All around us, legal requirements—known and unknown—swirl: opportunities and tripwires, rights and responsibilities. Though the basics of teaching and learning would appear free from the deadening hands of law and lawyers, such reveries are but wishful thinking. Especially in public education, we educators and parents are as much creatures of the law as are judges, legislators, lawyers, and regulators. We exist in a social universe ruled by law. And we put ourselves and our charges in harm's way if we deny that reality.

So I urge you to read this book as a matter of professional and democratic responsibility. There is no denying its importance. At the same time, I believe you will find within a powerful intellectual journey told with clarity and narrative purpose. The story of American public education law is the compelling fight resulting in *Brown v. Board of Education,* the quandary of religious devotion in a secular institution, the tension between authority and personal liberty, and the dual character of education as a progressive and conservative social force. In short, this text is not only a primer in American public education law but an instrument for informed civic participation.

Ramon Cortines
Deputy Mayor for Education, Youth and Families
Los Angeles Public Schools

CHAPTER ONE

The Cascade of American Public Education Law

Facts-and-Find

Law
any written, enforceable statement

This primer provides a brief introduction to American public education **law** for students, educators, and current or potential activists (meaning everyone). The first chapter, especially, is directed at the nonlawyer. No previous experience with the subject is necessary. The reader will be provided with a complete, if terse, foundation for understanding the American legal system as it relates to public schools. Each subsequent chapter will build methodically upon this understanding, topic by topic, so that in the end the scaffold will prepare readers to enter into active practice, not necessarily as attorneys but as serious, sophisticated, even dangerous analysts and advocates who can hold their own in the field through sound subject knowledge and agility.

Traditional education law books conform to the case law approach, long a staple of law schools. This has some advantages for budding lawyers but rarely will educators and activists—or most education lawyers for that matter—need to engage in the discipline of appellate argument taught through the case law method.

More frequently, professionals and the lay public will be presented with factually messy legal problems that never reach the **courts** and may have little to do with previous litigation. The problems might not even present themselves as legal matters at all, just everyday situations that require a discerning observer to identify as legal issues. Traditional case law books are of little value in identifying these situations or resolving them if no cases shed light on the predicament. Even if **precedent** exists, it may be far removed in time and **jurisdiction** from the current problem. Even knowledge of current **United States Supreme Court** doctrine is bound to be of little day-to-day guidance to those of us at the grassroots.

The aim and format of this book are meant to help meet daily challenges reacting to, or initiating, education law issues. Any lawyer will tell you that the facts of a current case are more important than an abstract **holding,** since the facts determine how a court or **administrative tribunal** will apply the holding. So this book emphasizes *facts,* in the form of very brief case studies, then guides the reader to *find* current law relevant to the situation in the reader's jurisdiction.

The place of facts in the life of the practitioner cannot be overemphasized. Obviously, an educator, student, or parent is most concerned with the facts of a particular legal situation that commands their attention. But advocates, too, are primarily concerned with facts; not only the facts of a situation that might be presented in the best light to a judge or jury, but the facts underlying precedential holdings. By artfully comparing the facts between cases, lawyers and other advocates can reveal similarities or differences between the cases that may have crucial legal consequences. The agility of comparing precedents according to factual similarities and differences—even wording a holding on the basis of a limited or expansive view of its underlying facts—is what many call

Court
a judicial body independent of the executive and legislative branches of government

Precedent
a controlling earlier judicial decision; however, what is controlling and what can be distinguished as precedent on the basis of the facts of the case may be a matter of dispute; see "holding"

Jurisdiction
the geographic or subject matter area within which a judicial decision is controlling

United States Supreme Court
the highest court in the federal system; the final arbiter of federal law, especially significant for its interpretation of federal statutes and the U.S. Constitution

Holding
a statement of law in a judicial opinion; however, what the holding actually is may be in dispute

Administrative tribunal
a court-like body presided over by a member or members of the executive branch, rather than the judiciary

"thinking like a lawyer." It is a skill well worth understanding, if not emulating.

The emphasis on facts has the added advantage of engaging readers in active analysis of how they might alter the fact pattern to their legal advantage. What policy statement, what initial response to the situation might alter the outcome? If traditional case law texts have their place in training lawyers for appellate argument, the facts-and-find method is appropriate for dealing in the moment of school and district decision making or advocacy. As civic participants, we all have a responsibility to become actively engaged with education decision making. This text provides the tools for such engagement.

Another problem with case law books is, not surprisingly, their emphasis on court decisions as primary legal source material. But judicial decisions are only one type of "law". New education **statutes, regulations,** and administrative rulings are generated with blistering speed in our country so that traditional judicial analysis can become a hindrance if it does not include synthesis with legislative and executive materials at the federal, state, and local levels. Think of the federal No Child Left Behind Act and related state law. Very few cases exist to guide us in understanding these mandates; yet they affect every public school parent and child, indeed the entire country, because of their reach into school finance, employment opportunities, and attention to demographic inequities.

Statute
enforceable law created by the legislative branch of the federal or state governments

Regulation
enforceable material drafted by an executive agency on the basis of statutory authorization

This text breaks new ground in providing readers with instruction in how to use such critical sources of law. All of the tools are here, including tutelage in how to find and use hard copy and online versions of state and federal statutory and constitutional documents, as well as regulatory, judicial, and administrative material. Helpful secondary sources will also be discussed.

There are other advantages to the facts-and-find method for an education law primer. The case law method is notoriously difficult. Ask any first-year law student. The book and movie *The Paper Chase* tells the tale of a law professor making mincemeat of his charges through the case law method. Here the emphasis is on clarity and accessibility. The method employed here avoids hazing and seeks to maximize comprehension, drawing readers into the wonderfully rich world of education law instead of driving a substantial segment of my audience to the latest DVD or video game.

Another advantage, and one that deserves emphasis, is the ability of facts-and-find to explore the lawyer/client relationship. These vastly different roles create inevitable tension in both counseling and litigation situations. Case law—essentially a judge-to-lawyer monologue—reveals little of this tension. Facts-and-find will aid professionals and lay people of varied backgrounds in working together with their attorneys. Educators, parents, students, politicians, attorneys, community leaders, and those from other backgrounds can profit from this text and, with a common understanding, can build stronger working relationships that will benefit children.

Finally, the case method should reveal to the nonlawyer that she or he has a role to play in the legal, as well as educational, aspects of a problem. In a democracy, the law should literally be an open book. And, as a lawyer, I enjoy clients who can identify legal source material, read it, ask good questions, and make educated decisions. Facts-and-find provides a fertile vehicle for exploring these legal research tools, including online databases, so that clients can become better consumers of legal talent and aid more fully in their legal representation.

After using this text, readers should also be able to think "out of the box," becoming better lobbyists and legislative drafters. Many educators leave the profession frustrated by legal requirements that they don't understand and that they find inimical to helping children learn. A unique feature of this primer is its inclusion of material on lawmaking and intergovernmental relations because, as an instrument of democracy, the law is there to be made as well as followed. People should feel that through their individual efforts and professional or civic associations the law can be changed, and that neither they nor their children should be hostages of judges, legislators, and other noneducator public officials.

Education law is basically a problem-solving exercise, using case law and other sources to reach just solutions that will result in respect and stability for our educational and legal systems. My hope is that this approach will move us toward that goal.

The Source of Law Cascade

The American legal system is the backdrop for answering any question in education law. This majestic system, simple in organization and wonderfully complex in operation, must be mastered in addressing legal issues and, once understood, will yield solutions to parents,' students,' teachers,' and administrators' most intractable legal problems.

For the lay person, the legal system is best understood as the set of enforceable documents that are relevant to a particular situation. It is often said that our country is governed by law, not people. This means that, to be enforceable, any requirement should be written and approved in a procedurally correct manner. The key to mastering education law is to find and even create this relevant written source material.

Cascade
a metaphor used in this book to describe the changing dynamics of legal sources and the judiciary in American law

Constitution
the highest law in the United States, either in the federal or state systems

To understand how this source material operates as a system, visualize a **cascade,** a series of waterfalls in which each stage supplements action upriver. Like a cascade, our system is constant yet ever changing. You can go to Niagara Falls (or our **Constitution**) anytime—it is always there, breathtaking and eternal. Yet the waters of the Falls (and interpretations and amendments to our Constitution) are always new, swirling in whitewater eddies that boggle the mind. This dynamic aspect of law is important to understand. It is always changing as new constitutional provisions, statutes, regulations, and executive or judicial interpretations swirl around the seemingly static rules. The responsible citizen will realize this and will know how to identify changes in the lasting geography of our legal system.

What are the stages in this legal Cascade? They are simple to remember: Constitution, statute, regulation, and **regulatory guidance.** And since we live in a system of separate federal and state governments, like parallel rivers, this Cascade is repeated in both the federal and state systems, as shown in Figure 1.

Regulatory guidance nonenforceable material drafted by an executive agency on the basis of its own regulations

Each stage in the Cascade must be consistent with the legal requirements of the stages above it. For example, a statute is "unconstitutional" if it is inconsistent with a requirement of the Constitution. A regulation must be consistent with the statute that authorized it as well as with constitutional precepts. Remembering this parallel Cascade is the key to understanding American public education law. This simple Cascade does not yet include local, district, or private legal instruments, nor does it include the courts. These important concerns will be discussed shortly, but first a clear understanding of the Source of Law Cascade is critical.

Federal and State Constitutions

The sources of all of our law are the written federal and state constitutions. The federal Constitution is the supreme law of the land, governing the acts of all public officials, including public school teachers and administrators. Unless permissible under the Constitution, no public act is legal.

While supreme, the federal Constitution does not govern all matters of public concern. Each state has its own constitution, which, while subordinate to the

FIGURE 1: THE SOURCE OF LAW CASCADE

Federal	State
Constitution	Constitution
Statute	Statute
Regulation	Regulation
Regulatory	Regulatory

terms of the U.S. Constitution, dictates the legal activities in that state.

Statutes

Statutes are also called "legislation" or just "laws". But each stage of the Cascade is a law—meaning that it is enforceable—and so this book uses the more technical term "statute" to refer to an enforceable instrument passed by a legislature (either Congress or a state body) and duly enacted. All federal and state statutes must be consistent with the federal Constitution, and state statutes must also be consistent with their particular state constitutions.

Regulations

Regulations (or "regs," with a hard "g," as they are fondly called) are detailed rules created by executive agencies to operationalize statutes. To have mastery of the regs is to know how the system really works. But the federal Department of Education and state Departments of Education cannot create regulations unless authorized by statute, and the regs must be consistent with their statutory authorization.

Like a statute found to be unconstitutional, a regulation that the courts find to be statutorily inconsistent will be nullified (remember the Cascade!). If a majority of the legislature believes the reg to be inconsistent with their statutory intent, they can fine-tune the regulation by passing new legislation that supersedes the reg. The concept of the Cascade can thus be used in a cat-and-mouse game by executive, legislative, and even judicial lawmakers intent on having the upper hand.

How Is Regulatory Guidance Like a Box of Rice-a-Roni?®

Once a federal, state, or local executive agency establishes a regulation, the agency interprets the formal language of the reg into lay person's terms to guide administrators' implementation of the new requirements. This "regulatory guidance" is made available to the field to aid compliance with the underlying statute and regulation. But regulatory guidance, unlike the constitutions, statutes, and regulations discussed earlier, is not "law." It is not, technically, enforceable. There is no such thing as a violation of regulatory guidance, as there are violations of regulations, statutes, or constitutional provisions.

Regulatory guidance, while official, is really like the plate of chicken fricassee (or whatever that is) on a box of Rice-a-Roni®. It is a "serving suggestion," published by the executive agency that drafted the regulation to help practitioners obey the reg. The difference, however, is that actions consistent with the Constitution, statutes, and regs are mandatory. Actions consistent with regulatory guidance alone, apart from its underlying legal foundations, are generally voluntary. You don't have to use the Rice-a-Roni® to make chicken fricassee, but if you want your meal to be a guaranteed success, Golden Grain suggests you follow its recipe on the side of the box. Similarly, educators do not have to follow regulatory guidance to the letter, but if they want to be sure of successfully navigating often-confusing regulatory rapids, they can be sure that the agency will find their actions consistent with the regulation if they follow the guidance.

Just as educators should periodically review relevant constitutional, statutory, and regulatory provisions, they should request and read regulatory guidance from federal and state education departments. The guidance is available from the agency that developed the reg and activists seeking help should ask for it simply as regulatory guidance or by asking the agency for all interpretative material concerning a statute including questions-and-answers, auditors' handbooks, checklists, and the like.

Educators who have a good reason for deviating from the guidance should do so, like creative cooks who decide to make paella instead of fricassee. But unlike the cook whose creative dish fails, the educator might be subject to charges of insubordination or administrative proceedings by an agency that believes that this independent action violates the mandatory prescriptions of the original regulation and/or statute.

The Place of Localities, School Districts, and Private Entities in the Cascade

Cities, counties, towns, villages, and school districts in the United States are all creatures of their state governments. In terms of the Cascade, the laws of these political subdivisions are subordinate to the laws of their states. So, rather than acting as a third parallel stream in our legal Cascade, they are really a tributary trailing off beneath the state regulatory "falls," but then cascading down through a new system of statutes (often called **ordinances** at the local level, or Board policies in a school district), regulations, and guidance, each requiring consistency with the level above.

Ordinance
local statute

This tributary of local and district legal material extends down to the school level. School disciplinary policies and other documents are properly understood in terms of the Cascade as enforceable regulations upon which authorities can take action (and which parents, for example, can use in lawsuits alleging either that action was taken inconsistent with terms of the regulation or that the terms are inconsistent with requirements higher up the Cascade).

Contract
enforceable agreement between two or more parties

Contracts, too, are part of the Cascade. Made between two parties, private or public, these are enforceable documents that must be consistent with all pronouncements above them in the Cascade. Thus, a contract between a school district and a teachers union, or between a private school and a parent, must conform to constitutional, statutory, and regulatory requirements, but only so far as those requirements pertain to private activities.

The Judicial Cascade

In most books of this type, judicial decisions ("cases") form the core of the content. So, strangely for a law text, the role of the courts and judicial decisions have not yet been discussed, nor do they have a place in this book's main construct, the Source of the Law Cascade of American public education law.

But in education law today, the courts have only a marginal, if sometimes crucial, importance. They are eight-hundred-pound gorillas and require accommodation when they take a role. But this role is relatively confined. Statutes and regulations are the dominant "law" in the world of public education, and the vast majority of legally relevant educational decisions take place outside of litigation. So most matters that require educators' legal insight are not especially enlightened by strained analogy to other fact patterns or to abstract legal holdings, often from nonbinding jurisdictions.

In some ways, the courts in education law are analogous to referees or umpires in sports. In sports, most of fans' and players' attention is on the game and the action of athletes in competition. The "ref" or "ump" doesn't get involved unless necessary, with their rulings having dual effect: one on the parties to the infraction, the other on how the game is played to avoid a penalty. Similarly, in education law the courts are usually on the sidelines as innumerable interactions take place among the "players": students, teachers, administrators, parents. Only when one complains in a formal manner do the courts enter the field, ultimately signaling their decisions. More importantly, however, the fact of the courts' presence—the possibility of their entry into the game—forces students, schools, and others to play by the perceived rules even without judges' active involvement.

Judicial rulings are based either on simple application of facts to the plain letter of the law or, in more complex cases, on interpretations of laws. The courts generally act as referees, interpreting the consistency of players' actions according to the rule book. Knowing judges' past interpretations of the rules is important, but cannot substitute for knowing the legal texts themselves, especially when relatively few situations gain judges' attention—and those often in a different jurisdiction.

Changing metaphors, when a judicial decision bears on a situation, people must be able access and understand the pronouncement to determine its influence on future actions, but overreliance on case law to the detriment of constitutional, statutory, and regulatory provisions is like the captain of the *Titanic* studying the horizon and ignoring lurking trouble beneath the surface. Judicial decisions may be the highly visible tip of the legal iceberg, but the real trouble comes from ignoring the vast submerged constitutional, statutory, and regulatory foundations.

The judiciary interprets constitutional, statutory, and regulatory provisions and applies them to the specific facts of a case. Rarely in education law today, the courts also determine some questions based purely on previous judicial decisions or "common law". In our era, the vast majority of courts' education law work is in interpreting and applying the written instruments of the Cascade. Almost all court decisions make reference to these written instruments and preceding decisions interpreting the same or similar provisions. Judges' reliance on case precedents sometimes gives the impression that there is no underlying written instrument being interpreted—but there usually is, and the wise reader will check these underlying sources even while reading the judicial decision. Sometimes, since the river of law is dynamic, a new instrument or subsequent judicial decision will have changed matters since the original decision was written, so always make sure you check the latest legal material available, including so-called **pocket parts** as described later.

Pocket part
an update to a statutory code, often placed in the pocket of an earlier hardback edition.

With this perspective, an understanding of the judicial system is necessary for educators to obey judicial orders. Just as Figure 1 serves to clarify the structure of American education lawmaking, a similar Cascade clarifies the structure of the judiciary, with the same parallel federal/state tracks and the same requirement of downward consistency.

As is apparent from Figure 2, the federal and state systems rely on similar hierarchies of judicial interpretation. In each system, higher court "holdings," or interpretations of the law applied to specific facts, are binding upon lower courts. So if a litigant appeals a lower court decision, the appellate court's determination prevails. Similarly, a precedent from

FIGURE 2: THE JUDICIAL CASCADE

Federal	State
Supreme Court	Highest court
Circuit Court of Appeal	Intermediate appellate court
District Court	Trial court

a higher court is binding on lower courts within the same jurisdiction.

But since trial level courts (District Courts in the federal system and bodies going by a variety of names in the different states) and intermediate appellate courts (Circuit Courts in the federal system) have only regional jurisdiction, the rules that they proclaim are binding only upon their jurisdiction. Outside the jurisdiction, the interpretation is merely persuasive and has no enforceability. Just as a Mississippi Supreme Court decision binds only people in Mississippi, a decision by the federal Ninth Circuit Court of Appeals, which covers California, Oregon, Washington, Alaska, and Hawaii, is binding only in those locales. State intermediate appellate courts usually bind only a small part of the state, since their jurisdiction usually covers but a small region within the state.

This regional arrangement can obviously lead to the strange circumstance that a single regulation, statute, or constitutional provision is interpreted in different, conflicting ways in different parts of a state or the nation. This, in fact, often occurs as courts grapple with novel questions of law. One important role of state high courts (called by different names from place to place) and especially the U.S. Supreme Court is to resolve these differences so that legal interpretations are uniform. But such uniformity takes time to develop as different jurisdictions reach different conclusions before, and if, the Supreme Court decides to accept an appeal from one of the cases. So, frequently there are conflicts among the Circuits. While this may be frustrating for legal analysts, the rule of a given Circuit prevails in its jurisdiction, making clear the operative precedent in any given place at any given time.

Finally, just as in Figure 1 there existed "hidden" tributaries of local, district, and private instruments, there exists a hidden tributary in the judicial Cascade made up of administrative tribunals such as district grievance machinery, special education procedures, and appeals to superintendents, Boards of Education, and state education commissioners. These sub-judicial tribunals are extremely important and their decisions are given great deference by the courts. The knowing reader will monitor these sometimes obscure decisions within the relevant jurisdiction with the same attention that others give to the U.S. Supreme Court. Of particular note in education, for example, are decisions of impartial hearing officers in special education cases. While obscure, they can be as important to the litigant parents and school districts as decisions by the IRS in an appeal of an audit might be to a taxpayer.

Legal Research

Standing at the bottom of these multiple Cascades—state and federal, instrumental and judicial—educators are bound to be daunted by the humbling confusion of so much *law*. And as discussed in the previous sections, like tourists at Niagara, depending on where the reader stands (Missouri or Tennessee, Northern California or Southern California, school district A or adjoining school district B) the law may be different! And if the educator stands there long enough, the swirling legal waters will change, so that yesterday's law may be different from today's, even in the same location!

The giddy, important fun of legal research is suppressing this sense of vertigo, centering on the here and now, then finding that first legal source which will lead to others, and aligning these findings along the Cascade so that a hierarchy of authorities is revealed.

Since so much of legal practice is based on finding the law, legal research is a well-plowed furrow, making the job for "civilians" relatively clear, if arduous. The difficult part is finding the furrow.

Once it has been located, related cases, statutes, regulations, and the like will be automatically turned up by citations or annotations contained in the original document. Most helpful will be a set of well-indexed annotated state statutes or a handbook of education law published by a state school boards organization or other professional association of lawyers and/or educators. Also helpful are the following brief, clear descriptions of typical statutory and case law citation forms.

Statutes and regulations are typically identified by a volume number, the abbreviated name of the state or federal code, and a section number (the section symbol is "§"). So "16 NJSA § 583" is volume 16 of the New Jersey Statutes Annotated, section 583. The annotations are cases and regulations that relate to the statute. Crucially, included in the back of that NJSA volume and similar state and federal sources is a pamphlet called a "pocket part," which updates the hardbound statute and annotations. Checking the pocket part should become an automatic part of checking statutes, since changes in the law since publication of the book may be critical to solving your problem.

Judicial decisions or "cases" are identified in much the same way. You will usually see the title of the case (e.g., *Brown v. The Board of Education of Topeka, Kansas*), followed by a number, then an abbreviation, and then another number or two (347 U.S. 483, 496). Don't panic! The first number refers to the volume number of the abbreviated case **reporter** and the following number is the page of the volume where the case begins. The last number, if it appears, is a reference to a particular page within the decision. Here "U.S." is the official series of U.S. Supreme Court case reporters and *Brown* can be found at volume 347, page 483. A "reporter" is a series of similarly bound volumes that publish, or "report," decisions from a particular court. Every state and federal court decision is published in one or more reporters. If a **string citation** of numbers and letters appears, that means that the citations for the case in

Reporter
book or a series of volumes that compile judicial decisions or the decisions of administrative tribunals

String citation
a case citation to more than one reporter

Shepard's
a research tool for tracking cases on appeal and providing subsequent citations of cases, statutes, or law review articles

more than one reporter are being stated. Case law can be updated using a publication and online service called **Shepard's** that records how cases fared on appeal and provides citations to newer cases referring to the original.

All federal and state statutes, federal and state regulations, and many federal and state cases can also be accessed from publicly available websites. Libraries, however, are still unsurpassed sources of legal materials. They are especially useful for their well-indexed collections and for the admirable services of reference librarians. Librarians are invaluable guides through the turbulent waters of the legal Cascade. Students and practitioners alike would do well to seek out and follow their advice.

The Internet has changed legal research forever. While librarians continue to provide crucial assistance, traditional law libraries are in some ways obsolete. Since they are in the public domain, routine primary source materials such as statutes, regulations, and administrative and judicial decisions are freely available online. Even some secondary sources can be found in this way, though fee-based databases (see later) may be best for law review articles and the like. In addition to school district and state education departments' websites and the federal Department of Education at ed.gov, all state and federal courts maintain a presence on the web where documents can be readily downloaded.

As a result, even huge legal case books are dinosaurs. A primer of this sort does not need to reprint dozens of lengthy cases and other resources cited within. Here, about a dozen cases, drastically edited, provide a taste of the treasures that can be found in the complete opinions. This is done for ready reference and to habituate readers to these critical documents. By typing the case name or other citation into a search engine, the full text and other supporting material are instantly accessible outside these covers. No longer dependent on authors' edited versions, consumers are free to read (or skim) the entirety of these documents for relevant information. This exercise is well worth the trouble since gaining facility at legal text reading is a necessary skill even for lay people dealing with public education issues and, since the law is based on detail, edited versions inevitably give short shrift to important information.

In addition to the websites identified earlier, throughout the text, and listed in chapter five, the following free websites are extremely useful and should be explored for their finer points: findlaw.com, law.cornell.edu, oyez.org, justia.com, hg.org, nsba.org/cosa, aclu.org, aft.org, nea.org, educationlaw.org, aasa.org, nassp.org, naesp.org, cleweb.org, pta.org, and ncpie.org. Proprietary databases that require a fee, such as westlaw.com and lexisnexis.com, are also useful and are often available through the web portals of public libraries, colleges, and universities.

Paralysis Is Not an Option

Teachers, like most people, tend to avoid controversy. And legal missteps can result in adverse publicity, disciplinary proceedings, even termination. So many readers, especially educators, come to this subject paralyzed, seeking a list of legal "dos and don'ts" with which to navigate their careers.

The earlier sections reject paralysis as an option and explain why a list of legal dos and don'ts is impossible. Action cannot be avoided and risk is inextricably tied to action. Further, because of the local nature of education law in the United States, what is legal in one district may be illegal in another. Because of the changeability of the law, what is legal one day may be illegal the next. And because so much of how the law is applied is determined by the infinite number of fact situations that may arise, no one can predict an answer until the facts are clear.

So rise from your paralysis! You are in charge! Facts in hand and ready to navigate the Cascade of American Public Education Law, you are the master of your own educational destiny. There is no hiding from the legal aspects of public education, but there is also no choice but to *act* with as much gusto and legal knowledge as possible.

As this primer moves on to applying the Cascade and other foundation information from this chapter, please remember that application of the law is infinite, depending upon its changing sources and changing fact patterns for its vitality. Staying abreast of the changing landscape is for professionals, but the ability to access and think about the law in specific situations is the democratic responsibility of us all.

Glossary

Administrative tribunal—a court-like body presided over by a member or members of the executive branch, rather than the judiciary

Cascade—a metaphor used in this book to describe the changing dynamics of legal sources and the judiciary in American law

Constitution—the highest law in the United States, either in the federal or state systems

Contract—enforceable agreement between two or more parties

Court—a judicial body independent of the executive and legislative branches of government

Holding—a statement of law in a judicial opinion; however, what the holding actually is may be in dispute

Jurisdiction—the geographic or subject matter area within which a judicial decision is controlling

Law—any written, enforceable statement

Ordinance—local statute

Pocket part—an update to a statutory code, often placed in the pocket of an earlier hardback edition.

Precedent—a controlling earlier judicial decision; however, what is controlling and what can be distinguished as precedent on the basis of the facts of the case may be a matter of dispute; see "holding"

Regulation—enforceable material drafted by an executive agency on the basis of statutory authorization

Regulatory guidance—nonenforceable material drafted by an executive agency on the basis of its own regulations

Reporter—book or a series of volumes that compile judicial decisions or the decisions of administrative tribunals

Shepard's—a research tool for tracking cases on appeal and providing subsequent citations of cases, statutes, or law review articles

Statute—enforceable law created by the legislative branch of the federal or state governments

String citation—a case citation to more than one reporter

United States Supreme Court—the highest court in the federal system; the final arbiter of federal law, especially significant for its interpretation of federal statutes and the U.S. Constitution

CHAPTER TWO

Student Issues

The average day in a public school would seem to be free from legal concerns. Buses arrive, attendance is taken, teachers teach, students study, administrators take care of paperwork, lunch is served, after-school teams and clubs meet. There is the general throb of instructional and social life. But beneath the surface, complex legal arrangements both dictate and react to the daily hum.

Bill of Rights
the first ten Amendments to the U.S. Constitution, encompassing basic personal freedoms and limits on government interference with those rights

First Amendment
the first provision of the Bill of Rights, which includes the rights to freedom of religion, speech, press, assembly, and association, and to demand government action

This chapter looks at a few of the legal issues that exist in schools, primarily as a result of the impact of the **Bill of Rights** on public schools, and especially those issues arising from the **First Amendment**. This is not to deny the importance of many other laws that affect the school day, some of which will be explored in later chapters. The bus company has a contract with the school district or the district runs its own transportation service, requiring insurance contracts. Attendance is taken, in part, to leverage state aid according to statutory formulae. Student enrollment is determined, in part, through constitutional and statutory antidiscrimination laws. Certain instructional content or methods are required by district, state, and federal mandates. Teachers have employment contracts, either through collective bargaining by their union or individually. Financing for the school building is necessary, as well as supply contracts consistent with required procedures governing public purchasing. School meals take place within an entire federal, state, and local regulatory structure to assure student nutrition and financial subsidies. Sports and other school programs are subject to health and safety requirements, and possibly rules for ascertaining student substance abuse.

Within this web of interwoven requirements, why concentrate on the Constitution? For the most part, this is a matter of practicality and tradition. There are so many areas that an education law text can cover, and so many variations from state to state, district to district, that it would simply be impractical to list all of the education law issues that might arise, let alone give coherent answers as to how each should be addressed. Amidst the almost infinite subject matter that arises in education law there can be limitless fact situations within the legal framework of thousands of different school district jurisdictions. So education law texts traditionally address the big picture, as defined by the supreme law of the land, the U.S. Constitution, as interpreted by the country's final arbiter of the Constitution, the U.S. Supreme Court.

This book follows its antecedents, then, by beginning its discussion of substantive educational law in the traditional manner, with school-based topics affected by the Constitution's Bill of Rights. However, rather than end there, the range is extended in later chapters to a broad sample of other issues better addressed as district, state, and federal matters. The organization is admittedly arbitrary but works to give coherence to the sprawling body of law that those in the field of education must come to master.

Of all constitutional provisions, why the Bill of Rights? Mainly because nowhere in the body of the Constitution's original seven Articles is "education" mentioned; hence, little of the Constitution directly addresses the concerns of public schools. We therefore derive most constitutionally driven education law from the first ten Amendments, the Bill of Rights, which are mostly concerned with individual liberties. Most other education law is statutory, and the vast bulk of that is left to the states to legislate. That is why a state handbook of education law is critical to the practitioner, but this text is more limited in its scope.

Many of these nonconstitutional issues will be addressed in subsequent chapters. For now, though, we start by exploring how the Constitution protects individual rights in public schools, balanced by courts' recognition that this key public institution requires an orderly environment, respect for educators' professional discretion, and, as an engine of democracy and socialization, vibrant community input through majority rule.

To introduce these topics and to help understand the practice of finding education law from a set of facts that might arise in an everyday school situation, a "facts-and-find" methodology is used to show how relevant legal material can be found when practitioners are presented with a unique set of facts. After all, that is how education law takes place in the real world and hence, it is the best way to tackle the same material in this text.

Expression

Facts

Kevin, a public high school student, often provokes the administration over civil liberties issues. Once, in response to an assignment to draw a political cartoon, he drew a picture of a priest captioned, "Reach out and touch someone." Another time, when students were asked to come to a school-sponsored event dressed as a famous person, Kevin dressed as Hitler. One Halloween, after students were explicitly told over the public address system to come to school in "proper attire" rather than costume, he dressed in drag: a below-the-knee floral skirt, matching scarf, blouse, jacket, panty hose, eye shadow, and lipstick. Kevin's outfit was remarkably like that worn regularly by the female school superintendent but emphatically not like that worn by his female principal, who often wore a suit and tie to work. Nonetheless, he was suspended for his act of defiance.

Find

"First Amendment rights, applied in light of the special characteristics of the school environment, are available to teachers and students. It can hardly be argued that either students or teachers shed their constitutional rights to freedom of speech or expression at the schoolhouse gate," *Tinker v. Des Moines Independent Community School District,* 393 U.S. 503 (1969). While the ringing phrases of Justice Fortas still apply today, they ring somewhat hollow. One question is whether Kevin's dress was a political act of dissent, deserving full protection under the **Free Speech Clause** of the First Amendment, or just a prank (which still might qualify for constitutional protection, though to a lesser extent). Another question, and here the facts are key, is whether Kevin's stunt actually disrupted the school's educational environment.

Free Speech Clause that part of the First Amendment that guarantees "freedom of speech," which has been interpreted to include any medium, though the freedom is not absolute, especially in the for public school students

On the basis of the facts, there is some question in the first place whether Kevin did anything wrong. Was the public address announcement enforceable or just advisory? Was it an arbitrary, procedurally infirm requirement outside the principal's authority or a rational extension of her legitimate powers in light of some problem that past costume-wearing had provoked? The school's dress code, assumed here to have been legitimately adopted and substantively constitutional, prohibits clothing that is "distracting" or advertises "sexual activity or preference." But was the outfit in question either a distraction or an advertisement of sexuality? Does it meet the test of proper attire announced by the principal? Perhaps a rule as vague as requiring proper attire is so overly broad as to give inadequate notice of impermissible conduct. Or is that hair-splitting? Don't we all just know what is appropriate and what amounts to a teenager's acting out?

According to the principal, the school did not permit cross-dressing, and "there would be some girls who would be offended" by Kevin's outfit. While the threshold of disruption required for the school to win the case is low, mere "offense" seems to be below even this standard. Indeed, the point of the First Amendment is to protect offensive speech; inoffensive speech is rarely quashed.

Thus, without some proof that Kevin's outfit either violated the dress code or caused actual disruption or the imminent threat of disruption to the school's educational mission, his outrageous conduct was probably permissible as a protected act of free expression. Many cases similar to this exist, from miniskirts to offensive T-shirt messages, and educators would do well to tread carefully—and to marshal their facts under existing, specific dress codes that avoid subjective terms such as "appropriate" or "proper"—before proceeding with disciplinary action.

At the same time, courts recognize that public schools are arenas where students will attempt to stretch limits and educators need to be able to enforce reasonable, and reasonably expressed, rules. In a landmark case, *Bethel v. Fraser,* 478 U.S. 675 (1986) the Supreme Court held that a bawdy campaign speech during a student election crossed the line, cited favorably in *Morse v. Frederick* ("Bong Hits 4 Jesus"), 06-278 (U.S. Supreme Court, 2007). What was the difference between *Bethel* and *Tinker,* cited earlier in this section? Some cynics would say that the difference was simply time—a more liberal Supreme Court deciding *Tinker* (1969) and a more conservative Court deciding *Bethel* 16 years later. But the facts were very different, too, leading to different conclusions and a roadmap for us to use in our own practice.

Tinker arose from student protest of the Vietnam War. Previously, the school district had allowed symbolic political speech in the form of candidate buttons and the like. But, threatened by the fear of political protest, the principals of the Des Moines public schools devised a specific policy to discipline the *Tinker* protesters, a few students wearing black armbands to class. Probably no policy would have survived First Amendment scrutiny in this case, since "abridging the freedom of speech" was clearly at the heart of the principals' action. But, importantly, the principals failed to follow district procedures for adopting such a policy, which required school board approval. Moreover, since no evidence was presented that instruction was disrupted, the protest seemed not to interfere with regular school activities.

In *Bethel,* however, a matter of decidedly lower public importance was clearly addressed by a properly approved, reasonable school policy that gave adequate notice to Fraser that his behavior—and the audience disruption purposely caused by his speech—would not be tolerated. That young children were in the audience during Fraser's sexually charged speech was also given weight by the Court, a matter that school administrators would be wise to cite in any similar circumstance.

This process of comparing precedents—and facts—is common in legal discourse. Through this comparative analysis, we find that there figure into courtroom calculations of the legality of student expression such factors as procedurally correct, explicit school rules; actual, imminent, or merely possible disruption; the nature of the speech itself; and the age of the audience.

Bethel School District No. 403 v. Fraser, 478 U.S. 675 (1986) [some text omitted]

Chief Justice Burger delivered the opinion of the Court.

We granted certiorari to decide whether the First Amendment prevents a school district from disciplining a high school student for giving a lewd speech at a school assembly.

I

A

On April 26, 1983, respondent Matthew N. Fraser, a student at Bethel High School in Pierce County, Washington, delivered a speech nominating a fellow student for student elective office.

Approximately 600 high school students, many of whom were 14-year-olds, attended the assembly. Students were required to attend the assembly or to report to the study hall. The assembly was part of a school-sponsored educational program in self-government. Students who elected not to attend the assembly were required to report to study hall. During the entire speech, Fraser referred to his candidate in terms of an elaborate, graphic, and explicit sexual metaphor.

Two of Fraser's teachers, with whom he discussed the contents of his speech in advance, informed him that the speech was "inappropriate and that he probably should not deliver it," and that his delivery of the speech might have "severe consequences."

During Fraser's delivery of the speech, a school counselor observed the reaction of students to the speech. Some students hooted and yelled; some by gestures graphically simulated the sexual activities pointedly alluded to in respondent's speech. Other students appeared to be bewildered and embarrassed by the speech. One teacher reported that, on the day following the speech, she found it necessary to forgo a portion of the scheduled class lesson in order to discuss the speech with the class. *Id.* at 41–44.

A Bethel High School disciplinary rule prohibiting the use of obscene language in the school provides:

> Conduct which materially and substantially interferes with the educational process is prohibited, including the use of obscene, profane language or gestures.

The morning after the assembly, the Assistant Principal called Fraser into her office and notified him that the school considered his speech to have been a violation of this rule. Fraser was presented with copies of five letters submitted by teachers, describing his conduct at the assembly; he was given a chance to explain his conduct and he admitted to having given the speech described and that he deliberately used sexual innuendo in the speech. Fraser was then informed that he would be suspended for three days, and that his name would be removed from the list of candidates for graduation speaker at the school's commencement exercises.

Fraser sought review of this disciplinary action through the School District's grievance procedures. The hearing officer determined that the speech given by respondent was "indecent, lewd, and offensive to the modesty and decency of many of the students and faculty in attendance at the assembly." The examiner determined that the speech fell within the ordinary meaning of "obscene," as used in the disruptive conduct rule, and affirmed the discipline in its entirety. Fraser served two days of his suspension, and was allowed to return to school on the third day.

II

This Court acknowledged in *Tinker v. Des Moines Independent Community School Dist., supra,* that students do not "shed their constitutional rights to freedom of speech or expression at the schoolhouse gate." *Id.* at 506. The Court of Appeals read that case as precluding any discipline of Fraser for indecent speech and lewd conduct in the school assembly. That court appears to have proceeded on the theory that the use of lewd and obscene speech in order to make what the speaker considered to be a point in a nominating speech for a fellow student was essentially the same as the wearing of an armband in *Tinker* as a form of protest or the expression of a political position.

The marked distinction between the political "message" of the armbands in *Tinker* and the sexual content of respondent's speech in this case seems to have been given little weight by the Court of Appeals. In upholding the students' right to engage in a nondisruptive, passive expression of a political viewpoint in *Tinker,* this Court was careful to note that the case did "not concern speech or action that intrudes upon the work of the schools or the rights of other students."

It is against this background that we turn to consider the level of First Amendment protection accorded to Fraser's utterances and actions before an official high school assembly attended by 600 students.

III

The role and purpose of the American public school system were well described by two historians, who stated:

> [P]ublic education must prepare pupils for citizenship in the Republic. . . . It must inculcate the habits and manners of civility as values in themselves conducive to happiness and as indispensable to the practice of self-government in the community and the nation.

C. Beard & M. Beard, New Basic History of the United States 228 (1968). In *Ambach v. Norwick,* 441 U.S. 68, 76–77 (1979), we echoed the essence of this statement of the objectives of public education as the "inculcat[ion of] fundamental values necessary to the maintenance of a democratic political system."

These fundamental values of "habits and manners of civility" essential to a democratic society must, of course, include tolerance of divergent political and religious views, even when the views expressed may be unpopular. But these "fundamental values" must also take into account consideration of the sensibilities of others, and, in the case of a school, the sensibilities of fellow students. The undoubted freedom to advocate unpopular and controversial views in schools and classrooms must be balanced against the society's countervailing interest in teaching students the boundaries of socially appropriate behavior. Even the most heated political discourse in a democratic society requires consideration for the personal.

The First Amendment guarantees wide freedom in matters of adult public discourse. A sharply divided Court upheld the right to express an antidraft viewpoint in a public place, albeit in terms highly offensive to most citizens. *See Cohen v. California,* 403 U.S. 15 (1971). It does not follow, however, that, simply because the use of an offensive form of expression may not be prohibited to adults making what the speaker considers a political point, the same latitude must be permitted to children in a public school. In *New Jersey v. T.L.O.,* 469 U.S. 325, 340–342 (1985), we reaffirmed that the constitutional rights of students in public school are not automatically coextensive with the rights of adults in other settings. As cogently expressed by Judge Newman, "the *First Amendment* gives a high school student the classroom right to wear Tinker's armband, but not Cohen's jacket." *Thomas v. Board of Education, Granville Central School Dist.,* 607 F.2d 1043, 1057 (CA2 1979) (opinion concurring in result).

Surely it is a highly appropriate function of public school education to prohibit the use of vulgar and offensive terms in public discourse. Indeed, the "fundamental values necessary to the maintenance of a democratic political system" disfavor the use of terms of debate highly offensive or highly threatening to others. Nothing in the Constitution prohibits the states from insisting that certain modes of expression are inappropriate and subject to sanctions. The inculcation of these values is truly the "work of the schools." *Tinker,* 393 U.S. at 508; *see Ambach v. Norwick, supra.* The determination of what manner of speech in the classroom or in school assembly is inappropriate properly rests with the school board.

The process of educating our youth for citizenship in public schools is not confined to books, the curriculum, and the civics class; schools must teach by example the shared values of a civilized social order. Consciously or otherwise, teachers—and indeed the older students—demonstrate the appropriate form of civil discourse and political expression by their conduct and deportment in and out of class. Inescapably, like parents, they are role models. The schools, as instruments of the state, may determine that the essential lessons of civil, mature conduct cannot be conveyed in a school that tolerates lewd, indecent, or offensive speech and conduct such as that indulged in by this confused boy.

The pervasive sexual innuendo in Fraser's speech was plainly offensive to both teachers and students—indeed, to any mature person. By glorifying male sexuality, and in its verbal content, the speech was acutely insulting to teenage girl students. The speech could well be seriously damaging to its less mature audience, many of whom were only 14 years old and on the threshold of awareness of human sexuality. Some students were reported as bewildered by the speech and the reaction of mimicry it provoked.

This Court's First Amendment jurisprudence has acknowledged limitations on the otherwise absolute interest of the speaker in reaching an unlimited audience where the speech is sexually explicit and the audience may include children. These cases recognize the obvious concern on the part of parents, and school authorities acting *in loco parentis,* to protect children especially in a captive audience—from exposure to sexually explicit, indecent, or lewd speech.

We have also recognized an interest in protecting minors from exposure to vulgar and offensive spoken language.

We hold that petitioner School District acted entirely within its permissible authority in imposing sanctions upon Fraser in response to his offensively lewd and indecent speech. Unlike the sanctions imposed on the students wearing armbands in *Tinker,* the penalties imposed in this case were unrelated to any political viewpoint. The First Amendment does not prevent the school officials from determining that to permit a vulgar and lewd speech such as respondent's would undermine the school's basic educational mission. A high school assembly or classroom is no place for a sexually explicit monologue directed towards an unsuspecting audience of teenage students. Accordingly, it was perfectly appropriate for the school to disassociate itself to make the point to the pupils that vulgar speech and lewd conduct is wholly inconsistent with the "fundamental values" of public school education. Justice Black, dissenting in *Tinker,* made a point that is especially relevant in this case:

> I wish therefore, . . . to disclaim any purpose . . . to hold that the Federal Constitution compels the teachers, parents, and elected

> school officials to surrender control of the American public school system to public school students.

393 U.S. at 526.

IV

Respondent contends that the circumstances of his suspension violated due process because he had no way of knowing that the delivery of the speech in question would subject him to disciplinary sanctions. This argument is wholly without merit. We have recognized that

> maintaining security and order in the schools requires a certain degree of flexibility in school disciplinary procedures, and we have respected the value of preserving the informality of the student–teacher relationship.

New Jersey v. T.L.O., 469 U.S. at 340. Given the school's need to be able to impose disciplinary sanctions for a wide range of unanticipated conduct disruptive of the educational process, the school disciplinary rules need not be as detailed as a criminal code, which imposes criminal sanctions. Two days' suspension from school does not rise to the level of a penal sanction calling for the full panoply of procedural due process protections applicable to a criminal prosecution. *Cf. Goss v. Lopez,* 419 U.S. 565 (1975). The school disciplinary rule proscribing "obscene" language and the pre-speech admonitions of teachers gave adequate warning to Fraser that his lewd speech could subject him to sanctions.

The judgment of the Court of Appeals for the Ninth Circuit is *Reversed.*

Discipline

But even if a rule is clearly broken, as in *Fraser,* can discipline cross constitutional lines, either because it fails to be procedurally fair or because it is overly punitive?

Where school officials go so far as to suspend a student, constitutional rules are clearly in play since the student is denied a **property interest** in his or her education and the stigma of such a disciplinary record may create a diminished **liberty interest.** Under the Fourteenth Amendment, these individual interests cannot be reduced by the government without "due process of law". That students have any **due process** rights under the Constitution came as something of a surprise when the Supreme Court decided *Goss v. Lopez,* 419 U.S. 595 (1975).

The facts of *Goss* are extremely material to understanding how these due process rights came to be recognized. Numerous plaintiff students were included in the case, which arose out of disruptions in the Columbus, Ohio public schools. But the lead plaintiff, Dwight Lopez, was not shown to have been involved in any disruption—even the cafeteria food fight, where he was merely "an innocent bystander." Swept up along with 75 students involved in the melee (which caused minor property damage but was otherwise of little consequence), Lopez was summarily suspended. As eloquently stated by Justice White, writing for the majority:

> The difficulty is that our schools are vast and complex. Some modicum of discipline and order is essential if the educational function is to be performed. Events calling for discipline are frequent occurrences and sometimes require immediate, effective action. Suspension is considered not only to be a necessary tool to maintain order but a valuable educational device. The prospect of imposing elaborate hearing requirements in every suspension case is viewed with great concern, and many school authorities may well prefer the untrammeled power to act unilaterally, unhampered by rules about notice and hearing. But it would be a strange disciplinary system in an educational institution if no communication was sought by the disciplinarian with the student in an effort to inform him of his dereliction and to let him tell his side of the story in order to make sure that an injustice is not done.

Thus was born the constitutional requirement of **notice and hearing** in public schools when a student is suspended for ten days or more (on the basis of Lopez's suspension for ten days; the rule could have been triggered by more or fewer days if the facts of the case had been different!). School districts and state courts have added all sorts of other procedural safe-

Property interest
the Fourteenth Amendment principle that people, including public school students, have a right to their legitimately gained property that cannot be limited by government without a formal process to justify the restriction; the right to a public education is a recognized property interest giving rise, in some circumstances, to the need for formal suspension procedures

Liberty interest
the Fourteenth Amendment principle that people have a right to personal discretion that cannot be limited by government without a formal process to justify the restriction

Due process
the procedures required in a given situation to avoid erroneous deprivation of personal rights (i.e., life, liberty, property) guaranteed by the Fourteenth Amendment

Notice and hearing
the constitutionally protected procedural rights of a public school student facing suspension for ten or more days to know the charge and to be able to give testimony about the circumstances giving rise to the charge

guards to prevent principals and superintendents from imposing unjust punishments on students, so it is important to review the discipline code and procedural regulations for your own locality. But, as a constitutional matter, all that is required to suspend a student for ten days or more is notice and hearing. Any lesser punishment is deemed to be constitutionally ***de minimis,*** in that it fails to rise to the level of a Fourteenth Amendment deprivation of liberty or property, and so no constitutionally mandated procedures are due.

De minimis describes relatively inconsequential infractions that do not require judicial scrutiny

Goss v. Lopez, 419 U.S. 565 (1975) [some text omitted]

MR. JUSTICE WHITE delivered the opinion of the Court.

This appeal by various administrators of the Columbus, Ohio, Public School System (CPSS) challenges the judgment of a three-judge federal court, declaring that appellees—various high school students in the CPSS—were denied due process of law contrary to the command of the Fourteenth Amendment in that they were temporarily suspended from their high schools without a hearing either prior to suspension or within a reasonable time thereafter, and enjoining the administrators to remove all references to such suspensions from the students' records.

I

Ohio law, Rev.Code Ann. § 3313.64 (1972), provides for free education to all children between the ages of six and 21. Section 3313.66 of the Code empowers the principal of an Ohio public school to suspend a pupil for misconduct for up to 10 days or to expel him. In either case, he must notify the student's parents within 24 hours and state the reasons for his action. A pupil who is expelled, or his parents, may appeal the decision to the Board of Education, and, in connection therewith, shall be permitted to be heard at the board meeting. The Board may reinstate the pupil following the hearing. No similar procedure is provided in § 3313.66 or any other provision of state law for a suspended student. Aside from a regulation tracking the statute, at the time of the imposition of the suspensions in this case, the CPSS itself had not issued any written procedure applicable to suspensions. Nor, so far as the record reflects, had any of the individual high schools involved in this case. Each, however, had formally or informally described the conduct for which suspension could be imposed.

The nine named appellees, each of whom alleged that he or she had been suspended from public high school in Columbus for up to 10 days without a hearing pursuant to § 3313.66, filed an action under 42 U.S.C. § 1993 against the Columbus Board of Education and various administrators of the CPSS. The complaint sought a declaration that § 3313.66 was unconstitutional in that it permitted public school administrators to deprive plaintiffs of their rights to an education without a hearing of any kind, in violation of the procedural due process component of the Fourteenth Amendment. It also sought to enjoin the public school officials from issuing future suspensions pursuant to § 3313.66, and to require them to remove references to the past suspensions from the records of the students in question.

The proof below established that the suspensions arose out of a period of widespread student unrest in the CPSS during February and March, 1971. Six of the named plaintiffs, Rudolph Sutton, Tyrone Washington, Susan Cooper, Deborah Fox, Clarence Byars, and Bruce Harris, were students at the Marion-Franklin High School and were each suspended for 10 days on account of disruptive or disobedient conduct committed in the presence of the school administrator who ordered the suspension. One of these, Tyrone Washington, was among a group of students demonstrating in the school auditorium while a class was being conducted there. He was ordered by the school principal to leave, refused to do so, and was suspended. Rudolph Sutton, in the presence of the principal, physically attacked a police officer who was attempting to remove Tyrone Washington from the auditorium. He was immediately suspended. The other four Marion-Franklin students were suspended for similar conduct. None was given a hearing to determine the operative facts underlying the suspension, but each, together with his or her parents, was offered the opportunity to attend a conference, subsequent to the effective date of the suspension, to discuss the student's future.

Two named plaintiffs, Dwight Lopez and Betty Crome, were students at the Central High School and McGuffey Junior High School, respectively. The former was suspended in connection with a disturbance in the lunchroom which involved some physical damage to school property. Lopez testified that at least 75 other students were suspended from his school on the same day. He also testified below that he was not a party to the destructive conduct, but was instead an innocent bystander. Because no one from the school testified with regard to this incident, there is no evidence in the record indicating the official basis for concluding otherwise. Lopez never had a hearing.

Betty Crome was present at a demonstration at a high school other than the one she was attending. There she was arrested together with others, taken to the police station, and released without being formally charged. Before she went to school on the following day, she was notified that she had been suspended for a 10-day period. Because no one from the school testified with respect to this incident, the record does not disclose how the McGuffey Junior High School principal went about making the decision to suspend Crome, nor does it disclose on what information the decision was based. It is clear from the record that no hearing was ever held.

II

At the outset, appellants contend that, because there is no constitutional right to an education at public expense, the Due Process Clause does not protect against expulsions from the public school system. This position misconceives the nature of the issue, and is refuted by prior decisions. The Fourteenth Amendment forbids the State to deprive any person of life, liberty, or property without due process of law. Protected interests in property are normally "not created by the Constitution. Rather, they are created and their dimensions are defined" by an independent source such as state statutes or rules entitling the citizen to certain benefits. *Board of Regents v. Roth,* 408 U.S. 564, 577 (1972).

Here, on the basis of state law, appellees plainly had legitimate claims of entitlement to a public education.

Although Ohio may not be constitutionally obligated to establish and maintain a public school system, it has nevertheless done so, and has required its children to attend. Those young people do not "shed their constitutional rights" at the schoolhouse door. *Tinker v. Des Moines School Dist.,* 393 U.S. 503, 506 (1969).

> The Fourteenth Amendment, as now applied to the States, protects the citizen against the State itself and all of its creatures—Boards of Education not excepted.

West Virginia Board of Education v. Barnette, 319 U.S. 624, 637 (1943). The authority possessed by the State to prescribe and enforce standards of conduct in its schools, although concededly very broad, must be exercised consistently with constitutional safeguards. Among other things, the State is constrained to recognize a student's legitimate entitlement to a public education as a property interest which is protected by the Due Process Clause and which may not be taken away for misconduct without adherence to the minimum procedures required by that Clause.

The Due Process Clause also forbids arbitrary deprivations of liberty. "Where a person's good name, reputation, honor, or integrity is at stake because of what the government is doing to him," the minimal requirements of the Clause must be satisfied. *Wisconsin v. Constantineau,* 400 U.S. 433, 437 (1971); *Board of Regents v. Roth, supra,* at 573. School authorities here suspended appellees from school for periods of up to 10 days based on charges of misconduct. If sustained and recorded, those charges could seriously damage the students' standing with their fellow pupils and their teachers as well as interfere with later opportunities for higher education and employment. It is apparent that the claimed right of the State to determine unilaterally and without process whether that misconduct has occurred immediately collides with the requirements of the Constitution.

Appellants proceed to argue that, even if there is a right to a public education protected by the Due Process Clause generally, the Clause comes into play only when the State subjects a student to a "severe detriment or grievous loss". The loss of 10 days, it is said, is neither severe nor grievous and the Due Process Clause is therefore of no relevance. Appellants' argument is again refuted by our prior decisions; for in determining

> whether due process requirements apply in the first place, we must look not to the "weight" but to the *nature* of the interest at stake.

Board of Regents v. Roth, *supra*, at 570–571. Appellees were excluded from school only temporarily, it is true, but the length and consequent severity of a deprivation, while another factor to weigh in determining the appropriate form of hearing, "is not decisive of the basic right" to a hearing of some kind. *Fuentes v. Shevin,* 407 U.S. 67, 86 (1972). The Court's view has been that, as long as a property deprivation is not *de minimis,* its gravity is irrelevant to the question whether account must be taken of the Due Process Clause. A 10-day suspension from school is not *de minimis,* in our view, and may not be imposed in complete disregard of the Due Process Clause.

A short suspension is, of course, a far milder deprivation than expulsion. But, "education is perhaps the most important function of state and local governments," *Brown v. Board of Education,* 347 U.S. 483, 493 (1954), and the total exclusion from the educational process for more than a trivial period, and certainly if the suspension is for 10 days, is a serious event in the life of the suspended child. Neither the property interest in educational benefits temporarily denied nor the liberty interest in reputation, which is also implicated, is so insubstantial that suspensions may constitutionally be imposed by any procedure the school chooses, no matter how arbitrary.

III

"Once it is determined that due process applies, the question remains what process is due." *Morrissey v. Brewer,* 408 U.S. at 481 (1972). We turn to that question, fully realizing, as our cases regularly do, that the interpretation and application of the Due Process Clause are intensely practical matters, and that "[t]he very nature of due process negates any concept of inflexible procedures universally applicable to every imaginable situation." *Cafeteria Workers v. McElroy,* 367 U.S. 886, 895 (1961). We are also mindful of our own admonition:

> Judicial interposition in the operation of the public school system of the Nation raises problems requiring care and restraint . . . By and large, public education in our Nation is committed to the control of state and local authorities. Epperson v. Arkansas, 393 U.S. 97, 104 (1968).

The difficulty is that our schools are vast and complex. Some modicum of discipline and order is essential if the educational function is to be performed. Events calling for discipline are frequent occurrences, and sometimes require immediate, effective action. Suspension is considered not only to be a necessary tool to maintain order, but a valuable educational device. The prospect of imposing elaborate hearing requirements in every suspension case is viewed with great concern, and many school authorities may well prefer the untrammeled power to act unilaterally, unhampered by rules about notice and hearing. But it would be a strange disciplinary system in an educational institution if no communication was sought by the disciplinarian with the student in an effort to inform him of his dereliction and to let him tell his side of the story in order to make sure that an injustice is not done. "[F]airness can rarely be obtained by secret, one-sided determination of facts decisive of rights. . . ."

> Secrecy is not congenial to truth-seeking, and self-righteousness gives too slender an assurance of rightness. No better instrument has been

> devised for arriving at truth than to give a person in jeopardy of serious loss notice of the case against him and opportunity to meet it.

Anti-Fascist Committee v. McGrath, supra, at 170, 171–172 (Frankfurter, J., concurring).

We do not believe that school authorities must be totally free from notice and hearing requirements if their schools are to operate with acceptable efficiency. Students facing temporary suspension have interests qualifying for protection of the Due Process Clause, and due process requires, in connection with a suspension of 10 days or less, that the student be given oral or written notice of the charges against him and, if he denies them, an explanation of the evidence the authorities have and an opportunity to present his side of the story. The Clause requires at least these rudimentary precautions against unfair or mistaken findings of misconduct and arbitrary exclusion from school.

There need be no delay between the time "notice" is given and the time of the hearing. In the great majority of cases the disciplinarian may informally discuss the alleged misconduct with the student minutes after it has occurred. We hold only that, in being given an opportunity to explain his version of the facts at this discussion, the student first be told what he is accused of doing and what the basis of the accusation is. Lower courts which have addressed the question of the nature of the procedures required in short suspension cases have reached the same conclusion. Since the hearing may occur almost immediately following the misconduct, it follows that as a general rule notice and hearing should precede removal of the student from school. We agree with the District Court, however, that there are recurring situations in which prior notice and hearing cannot be insisted upon. Students whose presence poses a continuing danger to persons or property or an ongoing threat of disrupting the academic process may be immediately removed from school. In such cases, the necessary notice and rudimentary hearing should follow as soon as practicable, as the District Court indicated.

In holding as we do, we do not believe that we have imposed procedures on school disciplinarians which are inappropriate in a classroom setting. Instead we have imposed requirements which are, if anything, less than a fair-minded school principal would impose upon himself in order to avoid unfair suspensions. Indeed, according to the testimony of the principal of Marion-Franklin High

School, that school had an informal procedure, remarkably similar to that which we now require, applicable to suspensions generally but which was not followed in this case. Similarly, according to the most recent memorandum applicable to the entire CPSS, school principals in the CPSS are now required by local rule to provide at least as much as the constitutional minimum which we have described.

We stop short of construing the Due Process Clause to require, countrywide, that hearings in connection with short suspensions must afford the student the opportunity to secure counsel, to confront and cross-examine witnesses supporting the charge, or to call his own witnesses to verify his version of the incident. Brief disciplinary suspensions are almost countless. To impose in each such case even truncated trial-type procedures might well overwhelm administrative facilities in many places and, by diverting resources, cost more than it would save in educational effectiveness. Moreover, further formalizing the suspension process and escalating its formality and adversary nature may not only make it too costly as a regular disciplinary tool, but also destroy its effectiveness as part of the teaching process.

On the other hand, requiring effective notice and informal hearing permitting the student to give his version of the events will provide a meaningful hedge against erroneous action. At least the disciplinarian will be alerted to the existence of disputes about facts and arguments about cause and effect. He may then determine himself to summon the accuser, permit cross-examination, and allow the student to present his own witnesses. In more difficult cases, he may permit counsel. In any event, his discretion will be more informed and we think the risk of error substantially reduced.

Requiring that there be at least an informal give-and-take between student and disciplinarian, preferably prior to the suspension, will add little to the factfinding function where the disciplinarian himself has witnessed the conduct forming the basis for the charge. But things are not always as they seem to be, and the student will at least have the opportunity to characterize his conduct and put it in what he deems the proper context.

We should also make it clear that we have addressed ourselves solely to the short suspension, not exceeding 10 days. Longer suspensions or expulsions for the remainder of the school term, or permanently, may require more formal procedures. Nor do we put aside the possibility that, in unusual situations, although involving only a short suspension, something more than the rudimentary procedures will be required.

IV

The District Court found each of the suspensions involved here to have occurred without a hearing, either before or after the suspension, and that each suspension was therefore invalid and the statute unconstitutional insofar as it permits such suspensions without notice or hearing. Accordingly, the judgment is

Affirmed.

Facts

A fourth-grade teacher's valuable ring went missing. Sure that a few of the boys in class had managed to slip it off his finger and hide it, the teacher wanted to forcefully discipline them. He asked the students to accompany him to an empty classroom during lunch, when the class was covered by an aide. Alone with them, he threatened to take them to the police and ordered them to strip to their underwear. After searching their pockets, he made them jump up and down in their underwear and patted them down. The ring was not found.

Find

This is based on a real incident and, though shocking, it could happen anywhere. Teachers sometimes lose it. So perhaps one way to not lose it is to analyze the legal aspects of the teacher's reaction. Were the teacher's actions illegal, rather than just unwise?

Search and seizure a government's limited right to search people and their belongings on the basis of cause

Fourth Amendment the provision in the Bill of Rights that guarantees, under certain circumstances, the right of individuals to be free of warrantless searches

Surprisingly, on the basis of the Constitution alone, the teacher may have been justified. The principle of **search and seizure** by government officials (including public school employees) is addressed by the **Fourth Amendment** to the U.S. Constitution: "The right of the people to be secure in their persons, houses, papers, and effects, against unreasonable searches and seizures, shall not be violated and no Warrants shall issue, but upon **probable cause**." Despite this constitutional protection, the U.S. Supreme Court has announced a

Probable cause
the standard for a search of a person by a government when criminal wrongdoing is suspected

Reasonable cause
the justification for public school officials to search students when there is merely a reasonable expectation of finding contraband; a lower standard than probable cause

lower standard for public school personnel, stating that **reasonable cause** can justify a warrantless search (*New Jersey v. T.L.O.*, 469 U.S. 809 (1984)). That means that the teacher did not need to get a search warrant if he had an articulable reason (not just taking a shot in the dark) to believe that particular students took the ring.

Assuming the reasonableness standard was satisfied, where might the teacher have gone wrong? Constitutional fidelity is not necessarily enough. In this case, checking district regulations would have given the teacher time to settle down, as well as throwing cold water on the planned search. Most districts strictly control teacher-initiated searches, fearing liability for assault and other charges, if not out of respect for students. In the district where the incident took place, a regulation explicitly states that "under no circumstances shall a strip search of a student be conducted." The regulation also sets forth detailed procedures, based in part on the age and gender of the student, for how any search is to be conducted and requires that the search be performed only by specifically authorized personnel, not teachers. This is a standard set of rules and should be checked against the specific requirements in your community.

A fact withheld in the original description, that the students involved were in a special education class for students with emotional disabilities, is not material to the legal prohibition of the particular search but should be noted by teachers involved in such incidents. The Individuals with Disabilities Education Act (IDEA), the current version of the federal special education statute sometimes still referred to as Public Law 94–142 or the Education for All Handicapped Children Act (EAHCA), curtails some disciplinary policies that might be legitimate for children without disabilities (see chapter four). These rules are complex and subject to change when the statute is amended by Congress, and so they are not detailed here. The point is that there are some issues such as student searches, special education, and even routine disciplinary matters such as suspensions that are so law-intensive that any activity in these fields should be checked for constitutional, statutory, and regulatory legality.

Another take on the search-and-seizure issue provides insight into political pressures that build as a result of decisions such as *T.L.O.,* cited above, where the Court found that public schools' reasonable searches of students without a warrant are permissible.

Facts

A congressional bill, the Student and Teacher Safety Act, would ease remaining restrictions on searches on public school grounds by school personnel. Citing Supreme Court precedents that give public schools the right to conduct searches of students on the basis of "reasonable suspicion," the bill would automatically define searches by full-time school personnel as reasonable if they arose from "colorable suspicion based on professional experience and judgment." The Act would extend to searches of student lockers and even personal searches of students and their belongings for drugs, weapons, and other dangerous materials. Failure to allow teachers to conduct such searches would jeopardize districts' funding under the federal Safe Schools and Citizenship Education Act. The bill was supported by the National Education Association (NEA), the nation's largest teachers' union, which, in a letter to House members, stated that the law would "help promote a safe school environment by requiring districts to have in place policies addressing reasonable student searches." After introduction by three members of the House of Representatives, the bill was referred to the House Education and the Workforce Committee.

Find

The bill is noteworthy for a number of reasons. First, is it really necessary or a matter of political grandstanding by Congress and the NEA? Beware the questionable attempt to align the bill with U.S. Supreme Court precedent. Does the bill square with precedent or stretch it? Since *T.L.O.* already legalizes reasonable searches, what is the value added in automatically defining searches for contraband "based on professional experience and judgment" as reasonable?

Progeny
decisions in later cases that rely on the reasoning from an earlier judicial opinion

A thorough reading of *T.L.O.* and its **progeny** is necessary to answer these questions. Mere review of the holding is inadequate to determine the proposed Student and Teacher Safety Act's fidelity to precedent. Advocates often skew their description of a holding to justify their point of view, wording it more narrowly or expansively than the facts of the case may justify. This is entirely ethical, but the wise legal consumer should not take such self-serving statements at face value. Judicial decisions are meant to be read, not merely summarized. A nuanced understanding of case law requires a review of primary sources to capture the complex interplay of facts and legal reasoning. Attorneys are expert at this, but lay people should not make case analysis the professionals' exclusive domain. The stakes are too high and democracy too precious to leave this valuable activity to lawyers alone.

Another important facet of the bill's text is that compliance would be tied to funding. Since the Constitution does not give Congress the direct right to legislate in the area of education, Congress frequently uses its funding powers to create substantive education law. This is true even in the gigantic areas of federal Title I funding (see No Child Left Behind in chapter four) and special education (chapter three), where huge federal, state, and local bureaucracies as well as complex regulatory structures have been created on the basis of Congress' funding power alone.

The lobbying effort by the NEA also deserves attention. Lawmaking is political, requiring multiple constituencies to ally in a common mission. Though the NEA is often aligned with the Democratic Party, the Student and Teacher Safety Act (catchy name, specifically chosen for its positive message) was a Republican initiative. Bipartisanship is often helpful in crafting winning coalitions. The strength of organizations, rather than unaffiliated individuals, is crucial. Make note of your own local, state, and national professional organizations and try to work through them in your own lawmaking struggles.

Also notice the procedure described by the facts: introduction by individual members of Congress and referral to the appropriate committee, a critical leverage point for supporters and opponents. The battle to gain introduction of a bill is only a first step. The favor of introduction should not absolve politicians from the duty of heavy lifting in committee and in the legislature as a whole. Ultimately, signing by the executive is also necessary, unless a legislative veto based on a super-majority (usually two-thirds or three-fourths) can be assembled.

Facts

Another example of lobbying for changes in the law concerns parents' political advocacy and organizing. When it comes to discipline, the problem can sometimes be in the eyes of the beholder. What is appropriate and what is inappropriate may be a matter of dispute among school officials, students, and parents. Where such disagreements are strong, formal access to law-changing apparatus may be necessary. One such example is demonstrated in the resolution and testimony shown in Exhibits 1 and 2, respectively, delivered when the New York City Department of Education decided that student cell phones were contraband.

Find

These examples of a formal resolution by a public body made up of dissident parents and their testimony before a legislative body should encourage those dealing with education law issues to challenge the legal or factual underpinnings of school district

EXHIBIT 1: RESOLUTION ON STUDENT POSSESSION OF CELL PHONES AND OTHER ELECTRONIC DEVICES ON SCHOOL PREMISES

Citywide Council on High Schools

Citywide Education Council

High Schools

Introduced May 10, 2006 and passed unanimously:

Resolution on Student Possession Of Cell Phones and Other Electronic Devices on School Premises

WHEREAS, the Citywide Council on High Schools is an entity created by Chancellor's Regulation D-160 to "advise and comment on educational and instructional policy involving high schools," and

WHEREAS, Chancellor's Regulation A-412 (V)(D-G) and the Citywide Standards of Discipline and Intervention Measures ("The Discipline Code") make it an offense for students to possess cell phones and other electronic communication devices on school property, subject to confiscation by school personnel under provisions of Chancellors' Regulation A-432; and

WHEREAS, cell phones and other electronic communication devices including music players are ubiquitous in society, useful and convenient for students en route to and from school, and, in the case of cell phones, important devices for maintaining student safety and communication between parents and students; and

WHEREAS parents throughout the city have expressed support for changing the current ban on such devices, especially in light of widespread and burdensome search procedures imposed on students as a result of safety concerns which do not generally relate to the matter of electronic communications devices but which are, however, confiscated incident to these sweeps for weapons and other dangerous contraband; and

WHEREAS other urban school districts have seen fit to permit students to bring electronic communications devices onto school property so that they may be used by students en route to and from school;

BE IT RESOLVED, that, the Citywide Council on High Schools calls upon the Chancellor and the Department of Education to revise Chancellor's Regulation A-412 and the Discipline Code to permit student possession or storage of electronic communications devices on school premises in order to facilitate their use by students off school premises, particularly going to and from school, and to provide schools with the individual capacity to regulate possession, storage, and use of students' cell phones and other electronic communications devices on school premises consistent with this resolution, in consultation with parents, teachers, students, and other members of the school community.

EXHIBIT 2: TESTIMONY TO ALLOW STUDENT POSSESSION OF CELL PHONES AND OTHER ELECTRONIC DEVICES

June 14, 2006

Testimony before the City Council Public Safety and Education Committees

To Allow Student Possession of Cell Phones and Other Electronic Devices in NYC Public Schools

On May 10th, The Citywide Council on High Schools voted unanimously to lift the ban on student possession of cell phones and MP3 music players in public schools and to put into place school-based practices to assure a safe and orderly learning environment consistent with this policy. The Region 10 High School Presidents Council unanimously supports our resolution. We are therefore grateful to the City Council for considering this measure and urge its passage, with the requested amendment that ipods and similar devices be added to the list of permitted items.

Parents expect schools to be orderly so that their children can study and learn. Parents also expect that they will be able to communicate with their children when they are not in school or during emergencies. Even ipods and similar music players are approved features of our children's often long journeys to and from school each day. These are not weapons. This is the standard gear of modern life. Students should be able to bring them to school. Safety and convenience demand no less.

We understand the Mayor's and Chancellor's position and we share their concerns. But the Department of Education's oppressive and overbroad prohibition is misguided and unenforceable. The City's "us/them" mentality regarding these non-dangerous items not only poisons the school climate but extends the government's reach into innocuous personal off-campus behavior.

Other major cities have seen fit to allow cell phones and other electronic devices in their schools. Indeed, under the informal "don't ask, don't tell" policy existing in most of our schools, these items remain unheard and unseen in tens of thousands of pockets and book bags throughout the school day.

Simply put, the Mayor and Chancellor are totally disconnected from parents and teachers on this issue. We need and want to talk to our children before and after school. The Mayor has no right to interfere with families' off campus freedom of speech and students' nondisruptive behavior! Consistent with the Chancellor's stated views about school empowerment, principal discretion and parent consultation, individual schools should make common sense rules to avoid disorder.

Mr. Mayor, can you hear us now?! If not, we are confident that the City Council will take the side of parents and educators by permitting our children to carry cell phones and ipods without fear of forfeiture. Thank you.

discipline policies when disagreements arise and satisfactory resolution is impossible using informal means. Litigation is sometimes worthwhile, but other methods should be considered, especially when policies are not necessarily illegal but public opinion is divided. Legislative activism in the form of lobbying, demonstrations, testimony, electoral initiatives, and the like constitutes a legitimate means of public action when laws seem unjust or misguided. Notice how the resolution references specific laws (in this case, Regulations of the New York City Schools Chancellor) that the parents want changed and how the testimony, in turn, references the resolution. Specificity is helpful when seeking such changes, so that lawmakers can be directed precisely in targeting their legislative weapons.

Leaving the lobbying and legislative aspects of education law and returning to the day-in/day-out activity of schools, we now investigate perhaps the most extreme of disciplinary matters, **corporal punishment.** Appalling situations are not as legally clear cut as they may initially appear. Corporal punishment is often misunderstood and requires dispassionate analysis, despite the urgency of the situation.

Corporal punishment discipline involving physical force, such as paddling

Facts

A student alleges that he suffered both physical injury and emotional distress after joining his public high school's interscholastic soccer team by being repeatedly roughed up by team members at the coach's direction. The student stated that the coach used this technique for discipline and to discourage him from remaining on the team. The parents of the student urged that the coach be brought up on charges of committing corporal punishment.

Find

First, it is important realize that the U.S. Supreme Court has ruled that there is no constitutional bar to corporal punishment in public schools. In *Ingraham v. Wright,* 430 U.S. 651 (1977), the Court stated that

Eighth Amendment
the provision in the Bill of Rights that guarantees, in criminal law, the right to be free of "excessive bail," "excessive fines," and "cruel and unusual punishment"

since the **Eighth Amendment** prohibition against "cruel and unusual punishment" applies only to criminal cases and because the plaintiff could bring a private action for assault, the school district was constitutionally permitted—though not obliged—to allow such a method of discipline. As a result, it fell to states and districts to define corporal punishment and when, if ever, it might be allowed. Approximately half of the 50 states have outlawed corporal punishment, and within states that permit the practice, many districts prohibit it. However, even where it is barred, the nature of the prohibition varies from state to state, district to district, and so local conditions and precedents are important.

This, then, provides an opportunity to engage in some close reading of a statute—a good skill to develop—while exploring how a real-world case alleging corporal punishment might be analyzed. In Virginia, for example, the corporal punishment ban states, as of this writing:

> § 22.1–279.1. Corporal punishment prohibited.
>
> A. No teacher, principal or other person employed by a school board or employed in a school operated by the Commonwealth shall subject a student to corporal punishment. This prohibition of corporal punishment shall not be deemed to prevent (i) the use of incidental, minor or reasonable physical contact or other actions designed to maintain order and control; (ii) the use of reasonable and necessary force to quell a disturbance or remove a student from the scene of a disturbance which threatens physical injury to persons or damage to property; (iii) the use of reasonable and necessary force to prevent a student from inflicting physical harm on himself; (iv) the use of reasonable and necessary force for self-defense or the defense of others; or (v) the use of reasonable and necessary force to obtain possession of weapons or other dangerous objects or controlled substances or paraphernalia which are upon the person of the student or within his control.
>
> B. In determining whether a person was acting within the exceptions provided in this section, due deference shall be given to reasonable judgments at the time of the event which were made

> by a teacher, principal or other person employed by a school board or employed in a school operated by the Commonwealth.
>
> C. For the purposes of this section, "corporal punishment" means the infliction of, or causing the infliction of, physical pain on a student as a means of discipline.
>
> This definition shall not include physical pain, injury or discomfort caused by the use of incidental, minor or reasonable physical contact or other actions designed to maintain order and control as permitted in subdivision (i) of subsection A of this section or the use of reasonable and necessary force as permitted by subdivisions (ii), (iii), (iv), and (v) of subsection A of this section, or by participation in practice or competition in an interscholastic sport, or participation in physical education or an extracurricular activity.

Under this statute, the coach's actions would seem to fall within the simple definition of "corporal punishment" under paragraph (C), and the fact that he did not actually touch the student seems immaterial, since the law does not require direct force but only, at (A), that someone "subject a student to corporal punishment," which seems to have occurred. A careful reading of the exceptions in (A)(i)–(v) does not seem to absolve the coach, since none of those circumstances seems to exist under these facts.

But (B) creates a huge loophole: if the coach made a "reasonable judgment" as to the need for punishment, the action is permissible! Also, at (C), in addition to the permissibility of "minor, incidental, or reasonable" physical contact under certain circumstances, there is yet another loophole for "participation in practice or competition in an interscholastic sport." All of these factors indicate a series of difficult evidentiary hurdles for the plaintiff.

The coach, too, may face some difficult legal problems. The greatest would be that, if the physicality was punitive on his part, most districts have highly prescribed processes for meting out corporal punishment. Common characteristics of corporal punishment policies include required notice, stages of disciplinary actions preceding imposition of physical contact, which officials are permitted to apply the punishment, what type of touching is allowed, parental consent, and the like. None of these factors appears to have been considered by the coach, at least as alleged.

That there are many questions about what actually happened to the soccer player is not surprising. Facts are often in dispute. That is why the notice and hearing requirement was introduced by *Goss,* cited above, and why the Anglo-American judicial system depends upon trials. Trials are basically mechanisms by which our society tries to determine the probable accuracy of allegations so that if there is a finding of culpability, the legal system can mete out punishment. Those involved in public education, whether parents, teachers, administrators, or advocates, need to have a degree of humility about their ability to know the facts of a given case before engaging in disciplinary proceedings.

Religion

A principal walks up to a huddled circle of six students kneeling in the hallway. Approaching them quietly, she peers into the group and sees that they're rolling dice with a stack of bills on the floor. "Thank goodness," she exclaims, "I thought you were praying!"

Few topics in education law are as charged and confusing as the place of religion in public schools and the place of public aid in religious schools. Using the common metaphor of a constitutionally dictated wall between church and state, these separate but related fact patterns can be seen as "doomsday walls," with advocates for each squeezing public school administrators from both sides, as in an Indiana Jones movie.

Establishment Clause the constitutional prohibition against governmental promotion of a particular faith or of religion over nonbelief

Free Exercise Clause that part of the First Amendment that guarantees freedom of religious practice

This condition arises from the First Amendment's two clauses addressing religion. The First Amendment states that "Congress shall make no law respecting an establishment of religion [the **Establishment Clause**], or respecting the free exercise thereof [the **Free Exercise Clause**]." The reader can ignore the word "Congress" in the Amendment and view the clauses as relevant to all public institutions since, by operation of the Fourteenth Amendment, the directive encompasses states and localities, as well as the federal government.

State action
government practice at any level

This places the concept of **state action** at the center of church/state analysis. Private individuals or groups are empowered by the Amendment's favorable treatment of "free exercise." In addition, they are not proscribed by the Amendment's limitation on state actors promoting religion. So keeping an eye on what the government is doing and what individuals are doing is key to understanding church/state doctrine as it relates to specific facts.

Facts

It's November and you are a teacher doing a unit on the Pilgrims. You ask five groups of students to write their own short dramatic presentations for a class presentation that will portray their persecution in England, their journey to North America, the first winter, help from Native Americans, and, of course, the first Thanksgiving. When you read the script written by Group 5, it is in the form of a religious service, thanking Jesus for His deliverance. What should you do?

Find

First, to restate the analytical framework, you need to identify the potential problem. Most important, are you in a public school? Only public schools trigger the state action limitations of the Establishment Clause. So if you are an independent school teacher or a teacher in a religious school, the First Amendment just isn't relevant, though you may be bound by internal school rules.

Next, assuming you are in a public school, what might be the problem with the prayer scene? Does it "establish" religion, meaning that it puts the public school—the domain of the government—in a position of becoming a religious institution in the eyes of the students? Obviously, people's opinions can differ on this. A good idea would be to check with the school administration to see whether a properly enacted school, district, or state regulation controls these facts. Remember, you are not supposed to know—it's impossible to know—all of the different laws that might be relevant under these facts, but you must realize that the facts raise legal questions and that the answers need to be found by reference to the Cascade and the research protocols that the Cascade engenders (see chapter one).

It is important under these facts to realize that it is the students who are praying and, indeed, who wrote the scene. The students are not government officials, so they are not bound by the First Amendment. The question becomes how much the school may have encouraged or even required the prayer through the assignment. On the other hand (a phrase lawyers love), is the prayer recited by the students, who are private individuals, protected by the Free Exercise Clause or even another First Amendment right, the right of free speech? Does it matter that they are reciting the words as part of a play script rather than actually conducting a religious service? Are all of the students completely voluntary participants? How could the teacher know? Also, the teacher might ask, is such a scene historically accurate? Just because the facts raise legal issues doesn't mean that instructional issues are negated.

Noteworthy in this discussion is federal regulatory guidance (remember the Rice-a-Roni® box from chapter one?) issued on February 7, 2003, by the second President Bush. "Guidance on Constitutionally Protected Prayer in Public Elementary and Secondary Schools" interprets the provisions of the No Child Left Behind Act. The guidance states that "where schools permit student expression on the basis of genuinely neutral criteria and students retain primary control over the content of their expression, the speech of students who choose to express themselves through religious means such as prayer is not attributable to the state and therefore may not be restricted because of its religious content."

How are you supposed to know all of this? You're not, which is why this is called facts-and-find, not facts-and-know. It's impossible to know because (1) there's too much, (2) it changes too often, and (3) very often application of law is a matter of opinion, based on informed judgment and collaborative thinking. One very helpful resource to find the February 7, 2003, guidance or other federal education guidance is the U.S. Department of Education's website, www.ed.gov, or its information hotline: 800-USA-LEARN.

Finally, on the basis of this analysis, what should the teacher do about the young Pilgrims? Though it may get lost in all of the legal analysis after conducting thorough research, the best practice is what seems most educationally sound in light of the legal findings. For example, if the teacher is sure that the assignment was "genuinely neutral," to use the words of the guidance, and is historically accurate, the student performance should be allowed to go forward, unless some superseding student interest (what if one or more of the students was bullied into participating?), instructional consideration, or state or local law precludes it. Though the teacher might want to remind the students that this is a student production, not a teacher-directed exercise, unwarranted fear of the legal thicket should not keep educators from fulfilling their basic instructional mission.

If the teacher—in concert with school and district administration—thinks the assignment will extend students' understanding of the unit, the legal issues should be identified, prophylactic measures responsive to legal considerations should be readied, and then the teacher should *do the job,* which is teaching. Remember, paralysis is not an option (see chapter one). Choosing to permit the activity or to deny it might each be criticized. So practitioners need to maintain their professional integrity by acting in their students' best interests within the limits of the law. Knowing the law should thus promote beneficial instructional practice, not discourage it.

Two cases involving church/state law illustrate how modern interpretations of the Constitution create dilemmas such as our Pilgrim example for public schools and policymakers. The first case, *Santa Fe Independent School District v. Doe,* 530 U.S. 290 (2000), concerns the ability of public high school officials to permit student-led, student-initiated prayer at student football games. In a 6–3 decision, the Court held that the school's involvement violated the Establishment Clause by seeming to promote religious expression, thus, in the Supreme Court's view, unconstitutionally taking sides in a constitutional dispute between people of different faiths or of no faith. In actuality, this dispute was so incendiary that the plaintiff, "Doe," desired anonymity because of fear of retaliation or ostracism by members of the defendant community.

Despite the attempts of the district to subject the prayer to student referendum and election of the student speaker, thus making it seem that private rather than public actors were responsible, Justice John Paul Stevens, writing for the majority, emphatically "refuse[d] to turn a blind eye to . . . [the district's] endorsing school prayer. Therefore, the simple enactment of this policy, with the purpose and perception of school endorsement of student prayer, was a constitutional violation."

Public school officials, then, cannot even infinitesimally promote organized religious observance among students, though the difference between this and mere permission may be slight. Allowing truly private observance, such as reserving space for Muslim students' daily prayer requirements, is likely to be a different matter, but the merest hint of public sponsorship or endorsement will be a death blow.

This line was clarified by the Supreme Court regarding the permissibility of religious after-school clubs existing alongside other noncurricular clubs in *Good News Club v. Milford Central School District,* 533 U.S. 98 (2001). *Good News* prohibited a school district's ban of meetings on school property by a "quintessentially religious" organization, even while the district permitted meetings of the Girl Scouts and 4-H Club. The Court held that the prohibition violated the Free Speech Clause of the First Amendment and that no Establishment Clause violation would result. This precedent is at least partially **codified** in the federal Equal Access Act, 20 U.S.C. §§ 4071–4074, which prohibits public secondary schools from content-based discrimination when they create a **limited open forum** by allowing noncurricular club meetings. This means that not only religiously based clubs (whether mainstream or nontraditional) have access to the school, but also other types of affiliations: gay/lesbian/transgender clubs, hobby clubs, and the like. Before *Good News,* the Court in *Lamb's Chapel v. Center Moriches,* 508 U.S. 384 (1993), held that where a school board leased space to outside organizations, there was no Establishment Clause prohibition against its leasing to a religious congregation.

Codify
create a statute to reflect a policy or court decision, thus placing the law within a set of statutes, or "code"

Limited open forum
a First Amendment concept in which a public school opens itself to certain outside organizations and/or opinions, and is thus barred from discriminating against participation by other organizations or opinions based on their point of view.

Thus, while limited to facts concerning school endorsement of religion rather than its neutral treatment in the context of secular school policies, the wall between church and state on public school grounds remains, in the late Justice Hugo Black's phrase, "tall and impregnable." Those who desire public school support for religious practice are out of luck. It is a jolt to realize that not even a strongly conservative Court will crack this part of the wall.

But while those hoping for more favorable treatment concerning students' public religious practice will not get satisfaction, they will get spiritual and financial satisfaction in the nation's religious schools. In another landmark church/state case, *Mitchell v. Helms,* 530 U.S. 793 (2000), the Supreme Court **overruled** its own precedents to hold that religiously neutral instructional materials, such as computers and software, can be provided by the government to religious schools despite the possibility that those schools might divert the assistance to sectarian purposes.

Overrule
to negate a prior ruling or request; in the case of the U.S. Supreme Court, to reverse a prior holding

Plurality opinion
when no majority opinion is issued by the U.S. Supreme Court, the opinion of the largest group of justices (at least two but fewer than five) prevailing in a particular case

In a **plurality opinion** written by Justice Thomas, the Court rejected arguments that the government aid was unconstitutional because it provided indirect aid to religious activities and was divertible to religious instruction. The plurality determined that the aid was directed at the religious school students, not the religious institution, thus **curing** any Establishment Clause issues. Publicly financed vouchers and tax deductions for religious school tuition are also available under the holdings of *Zelman v. Simmons-Harris,* 536 U.S. 639 (2002), and *Mueller v. Allen,* 463 U.S. 388 (1983), respectively.

Curing
the process of modifying a document or practice to conform to legal requirements

As a result of the expansive analysis of *Mueller, Mitchell,* and *Zelman,* the gates are now largely open to government provision of tuition-based financing and of staff and materials to teach secular subjects in religious schools. As explained in a concurring opinion by Justice Sandra Day O'Connor, such government aid passes scrutiny under the First Amendment as long as the assistance (1) has a secular purpose, (2) is provided neutrally to public and nonpublic schools, (3) does not directly aid in teaching religion, and (4) does not result in excessive entanglement between church and state.

Lemon test
a three-pronged method of Establishment Clause analysis, now out of favor, that attempts to discern constitutional behavior according to the practice's purpose, process, and result

This is a twenty-first century spin on the **Lemon Test,** which is based on the case *Lemon v. Kurtzman,* 403 U.S. 602 (1971). *Lemon* established a famous three-pronged test for evaluating the constitutionality of state action regarding religion: (1) Is there a secular purpose? (2) Does the action promote or discourage religion? and (3) Does the action require excessive entanglement between government and religious institutions? The test has been legitimately criticized as giving an objective appearance to what is really a wholly subjective analysis—each question can be answered entirely on the basis of the judge's desired result. So it has been largely abandoned. But despite its analytic weakness and the Court's more recent emphasis on **neutrality** as the key pivot for church/state analysis, *Lemon* remains an omnipresent, if no longer an omnipotent, force in church/state law.

Neutrality
the currently prevailing concept in Establishment Clause jurisprudence that requires that government neither favor nor disfavor religious practice in policies and practices

Taken together, then, the *Santa Fe* and *Mitchell* decisions can be viewed as creating a judicial gate-keeping role so that public schools seem ever more hostile to organized public religious expression but allowing private schools to receive additional public assistance for their secular instruction and incidental services, such as math, science, standardized testing, and transportation. This can be seen as being in tension with the current executive tendency, as evidenced by the Bush administration's regulatory guidance on school prayer, to open public school gates to sectarian activities.

In the realm of public support for religious schools, tuition and private donations need now support only part of the school's mission. With increased government aid, private school administrators can decide to reduce tuition or increase services, in either case making their schools more attractive to public school parents, especially those seeking school support for religious activity.

Developments since the Santa Fe and Mitchell cases bear out administrators' continuing difficulties in dealing with the decisions' fallout. For example, many a high school football player uses the school's microphone to ask the crowd to join in a voluntary prayer. "Is it just the microphone that makes the difference?" asked the school district. Or, when announcing other community events, must principals exclude mentioning a "Rally Round the Flag Pole" prayer meeting outside the school? Would having a student make the announcement solve the problem of perceived church/state endorsement?

These and hundreds of other unresolved questions show how the constitutional walls continue to move inward on the public schools. As much as these changes might be ascribed to the vagaries of the Supreme Court appointment process, this evolution is not merely the result of presidential politics. It develops from important constitutional principles of freedom and tolerance, as well as from similar tensions within our national character.

Mitchell v. Helms, 530 U.S. 793 (2000) [some text omitted]

Justice Thomas announced the judgment of the Court and delivered an opinion, in which The Chief Justice, Justice Scalia, and Justice Kennedy join.

As part of a longstanding school aid program known as Chapter 2, the Federal Government distributes funds to state and local governmental agencies, which in turn lend educational materials and equipment to public and private schools, with the enrollment of each participating school determining the amount of aid that it receives. The question is whether Chapter 2, as applied in Jefferson Parish, Louisiana, is a law respecting an establishment of religion, because many of the private schools receiving Chapter 2 aid in that parish are religiously affiliated. We hold that Chapter 2 is not such a law.

I

A

Chapter 2 of the Education Consolidation and Improvement Act of 1981has its origins in the Elementary and Secondary Education Act of 1965 (ESEA) and is a close cousin of the provision of the ESEA that we recently considered in *Agostini* v. *Felton,* 521 U.S. 203 (1997). Like the provision at issue in *Agostini,* Chapter 2 channels federal funds to local educational agencies (LEA's), which are usually public school districts, via state educational agencies (SEA's), to implement programs to assist children in elementary and secondary schools. Among other things, Chapter 2 provides aid

> for the acquisition and use of instructional and educational materials, including library services and materials (including media materials), assessments, reference materials, computer software and hardware for instructional use, and other curricular materials. 20 U.S.C. § 7351(b)(2).

LEA's and SEA's must offer assistance to both public and private schools (although any private school must be nonprofit). §§7312(a), 7372(a)(1). Participating private schools receive Chapter 2 aid based on the number of children enrolled in each school, see §7372(a)(1), and allocations of Chapter 2 funds for those schools must generally be "equal (consistent with the number of children to be served) to expenditures for programs . . . for children enrolled in the public schools of the [LEA]," §7372(b). LEA's must in all cases "assure equitable participation" of the children of private schools "in the purposes and benefits" of Chapter 2. §7372(a)(1); see §7372(b). Further, Chapter 2 funds may only "supplement and, to the extent practical, increase the level of funds that would . . . be made available from non-Federal sources." §7371(b). LEA's and SEA's may not operate their programs "so as to supplant funds from non-Federal sources."

Several restrictions apply to aid to private schools. Most significantly, the "services, materials, and equipment" provided to private schools must be "secular, neutral, and nonideological." §7372(a)(1). In addition, private schools may not acquire control of Chapter 2 funds or title to Chapter 2 materials, equipment, or property. §7372(c)(1). A private school receives the materials and equipment listed in §7351(b)(2) by submitting to the LEA an application detailing which items the school seeks and how it will use them; the LEA, if it approves the application, purchases those items from the school's allocation of funds, and then lends them to that school.

In Jefferson Parish (the Louisiana governmental unit at issue in this case), as in Louisiana as a whole, private schools have primarily used their allocations for nonrecurring expenses, usually materials and equipment. In the 1986–1987 fiscal year, for example, 44% of the money budgeted for private schools in Jefferson Parish was spent by LEA's for acquiring library and media materials, and 48% for instructional equipment. Among the materials and equipment provided have been library books, computers, and computer software, and also slide and movie projectors, overhead projectors, television sets, tape recorders, VCR's, projection screens, laboratory equipment, maps, globes, filmstrips, slides, and cassette recordings.

It appears that, in an average year, about 30% of Chapter 2 funds spent in Jefferson Parish are allocated for private schools. For the 1985–1986 fiscal year, 41 private schools participated in Chapter 2. For the following year, 46 participated, and the participation level has remained relatively constant since then. See App. 132a. Of these 46, 34 were Roman Catholic; 7 were otherwise religiously affiliated; and 5 were not religiously affiliated.

II

The Establishment Clause of the First Amendment dictates that "Congress shall make no law respecting an establishment of religion." In the over 50 years since *Everson,* we have consistently struggled to apply these simple words in the context of governmental aid to religious schools. As we admitted in *Tilton* v. *Richardson,* 403 U.S. 672 (1971), "candor compels the acknowledgment that we can only dimly perceive the boundaries of permissible government activity in this sensitive area." *Id.,* at 678 (plurality opinion); see *id.,* at 671 (White, J., concurring in judgment).

In *Agostini,* however, we brought some clarity to our case law, by overruling two anomalous precedents (one in whole, the other in part) and by consolidating some of our previously disparate considerations under a revised test. Whereas in *Lemon* we had considered whether a statute (1) has a secular purpose, (2) has a primary effect of advancing or inhibiting religion, or (3) creates an excessive entanglement between government and religion, see 403 U.S., at 612–613, in *Agostini* we modified *Lemon* for purposes of evaluating aid to schools and examined only the first and second factors, see 521 U.S., at 222–223. We acknowledged that our cases discussing excessive entanglement had applied many of the same considerations as had our cases discussing primary effect, and we therefore recast *Lemon*'s entanglement inquiry as simply one criterion relevant to determining a statute's effect. *Agostini, supra,* at 232–233. We also acknowledged that our cases had pared somewhat the factors that could justify a finding of excessive entanglement. 521 U.S., at 233–234. We then set out revised criteria for determining the effect of a statute:

> To summarize, New York City's Title I program does not run afoul of any of three primary criteria we currently use to evaluate whether government aid has the effect of advancing religion: It does not result in governmental indoctrination; define its recipients by reference to religion; or create an excessive entanglement.

Id., at 234.

In this case, our inquiry under *Agostini*'s purpose and effect test is a narrow one. Because respondents do not challenge the District Court's holding that Chapter 2 has a secular purpose, and because the Fifth Circuit also did not question that holding, cf. 151 F.3d, at 369, n. 17, we will consider only Chapter 2's effect. Further, in determining that effect, we will consider only the first two *Agostini* criteria, since neither respondents nor the Fifth Circuit has questioned the District Court's holding that Chapter 2 does not create an excessive entanglement. Considering Chapter 2 in light of our more recent case law, we conclude that it neither results in religious indoctrination by the government nor defines its recipients by reference to religion. We therefore hold that Chapter 2 is not a "law respecting an establishment of religion." In so holding, we acknowledge what both the Ninth and Fifth Circuits saw was inescapable—

Meek and *Wolman* are anomalies in our case law. We therefore conclude that they are no longer good law.

III

Applying the two relevant *Agostini* criteria, we see no basis for concluding that Jefferson Parish's Chapter 2 program "has the effect of advancing religion." *Agostini, supra*, at 234. Chapter 2 does not result in governmental indoctrination, because it determines eligibility for aid neutrally, allocates that aid based on the private choices of the parents of schoolchildren, and does not provide aid that has an impermissible content. Nor does Chapter 2 define its recipients by reference to religion.

Taking the second criterion first, it is clear that Chapter 2 aid "is allocated on the basis of neutral, secular criteria that neither favor nor disfavor religion, and is made available to both religious and secular beneficiaries on a nondiscriminatory basis." Agostini, supra, at 231. Aid is allocated based on enrollment: "Private schools receive Chapter 2 materials and equipment based on the per capita number of students at each school," Walker, 46 F.3d, at 1464, and allocations to private schools must "be equal (consistent with the number of children to be served) to expenditures for programs under this subchapter for children enrolled in the public schools of the [LEA]," 20 U.S.C. § 7372(b). LEA's must provide Chapter 2 materials and equipment for the benefit of children in private schools "[t]o the extent consistent with the number of children in the school district of [an LEA] . . . who are enrolled in private nonprofit elementary and secondary schools." §7372(a)(1). See App. to Pet. for Cert. 87a (District Court, recounting testimony of head of Louisiana's Chapter 2 program that LEA's are told that "'for every dollar you spend for the public school student, you spend the same dollar for the non-public school student'"); §§7372(a)(1) and (b) (children in private schools must receive "equitable participation"). The allocation criteria therefore create no improper incentive. Chapter 2 does, by statute, deviate from a pure per capita basis for allocating aid to LEA's, increasing the per-pupil allocation based on the number of children within an LEA who are from poor families, reside in poor areas, or reside in rural areas. §§7312(a)–(b). But respondents have not contended, nor do we have any reason to think, that this deviation in the allocation to the LEA's leads to deviation in the allocation among schools within each LEA, see §§7372(a)–(b), and, even if it did, we would not presume that such a deviation created any incentive one way or the other with regard to religion.

Chapter 2 also satisfies the first *Agostini* criterion. The program makes a broad array of schools eligible for aid without regard to their religious affiliations or lack thereof. §7372; see §7353(a)(3). We therefore have no difficulty concluding that Chapter 2 is neutral with regard to religion. See *Agostini, supra,* at 225–226. Chapter 2 aid also, like the aid in *Agostini, Zobrest,* and *Witters,* reaches participating schools only "as a consequence of private decisionmaking." *Agostini, supra,* at 222. Private decisionmaking controls because of the per capita allocation scheme, and those decisions are independent because of the program's neutrality. See 521 U.S. at 226. It is the students and their parents—not the government—who, through their choice of school, determine who receives Chapter 2 funds. The aid follows the child.

Because Chapter 2 aid is provided pursuant to private choices, it is not problematic that one could fairly describe Chapter 2 as providing "direct" aid. The materials and equipment provided under Chapter 2 are presumably used from time to time by entire classes rather than by individual students (although individual students are likely the chief consumers of library books and, perhaps, of computers and computer software), and students themselves do not need to apply for Chapter 2 aid in order for their schools to receive it, but, as we explained in *Agostini,* these traits are not constitutionally significant or meaningful. See *id.,* at 228–229. Nor, for reasons we have already explained, is it of constitutional significance that the schools themselves, rather than the students, are the bailees of the Chapter 2 aid. The ultimate beneficiaries of Chapter 2 aid are the students who attend the schools that receive that aid, and this is so regardless of whether individual students lug computers to school each day or, as Jefferson Parish has more sensibly provided, the schools receive the computers. Like the Ninth Circuit, and unlike the dissent, *post,* at 22, we "see little difference in loaning science kits to students who then bring the kits to school as opposed to loaning science kits to the school directly." *Walker, supra,* at 1468, n. 16; see *Allen,* 392 U.S., at 244, n. 6.

Finally, Chapter 2 satisfies the first *Agostini* criterion because it does not provide to religious schools aid that has an impermissible content. The statute explicitly bars anything of the sort, providing that all Chapter 2 aid for the benefit of children in private schools shall be "secular, neutral, and nonideological," §7372(a)(1), and the record indicates that the Louisiana SEA and the Jefferson Parish LEA have faithfully enforced this requirement insofar as relevant to this case. The chief aid at issue is computers, computer software, and library books. The computers presumably have no preexisting content, or at least none that would be impermissible for use in public schools. Respondents do not contend otherwise. Respondents also offer no evidence that religious schools have received software from the government that has an impermissible content.

There is evidence that equipment has been, or at least easily could be, diverted for use in religious classes. Justice O'Connor, however, finds the safeguards against diversion adequate to prevent and detect actual diversion. The safeguards on which she relies reduce to three: (1) signed assurances that Chapter 2 aid will be used only for secular, neutral, and nonideological purposes, (2) monitoring visits, and (3) the requirement that equipment be labeled as belonging to Chapter 2. As to the first, Justice O'Connor rightly places little reliance on it. As to the second, monitoring by SEA and LEA officials is highly unlikely to prevent or catch diversion. As to the third, compliance with the labeling requirement is haphazard, see App. 113a, and, even if the requirement were followed, we fail to see how a label prevents diversion. In addition, we agree with the dissent that there is evidence of actual diversion and that, were the safeguards anything other than anemic, there would almost certainly be more such evidence. In any event, the evidence of actual diversion and the weakness of the safeguards against actual diversion are not relevant to the constitutional inquiry, whatever relevance they may have under the statute and regulations.

IV

In short, Chapter 2 satisfies both the first and second primary criteria of *Agostini.* It therefore does not have the effect of advancing religion. For the same reason, Chapter 2 also "cannot reasonably be viewed as an endorsement of religion," *Agostini, supra,* at 235. Accordingly, we hold that Chapter 2 is not a law respecting an establishment of religion. Jefferson Parish need not exclude religious schools from its Chapter 2 program. To the extent that *Meek* and *Wolman* conflict with this holding, we overrule them.

Our conclusion regarding *Meek* and *Wolman* should come as no surprise. The Court as early as *Wolman* itself left no doubt that *Meek* and *Allen* were irreconcilable, see 433 U.S., at 251, n. 18, and we have repeatedly reaffirmed *Allen* since then, see, *e.g., Agostini, supra,* at 231. (In fact, *Meek,* in discussing the materials-and-equipment program, did not even cite *Allen.* See *Meek,* 421 U.S., at 363–366.) Less than three years after *Wolman,* we explained that *Meek* did not, despite appearances, hold that "all loans of secular instructional material and equipment inescapably have the effect of direct advancement of religion." *Regan,* 444 U.S., at 661–662 (internal quotation marks omitted). Then, in *Mueller,* we conceded that the aid at issue in *Meek* and *Wolman* did "resembl[e], in many respects," the aid that we had upheld in *Everson* and *Allen.* 463 U.S., at 393, and n. 3; see *id.,* at 402, n. 10; see also *id.,* at 415 (Marshall, J., dissenting) (viewing *Allen* as incompatible with *Meek* and *Wolman,* and the distinction between textbooks and other instructional materials as "simply untenable"). Most recently, *Agostini,* in rejecting *Ball*'s assumption that "all government aid that directly assists the educational function of religious schools is invalid," *Agostini, supra,* at 225, necessarily rejected a large portion (perhaps all, see *Ball,* 473 U.S., at 395) of the reasoning of *Meek* and *Wolman* in invalidating the lending of materials and equipment, for *Ball* borrowed that assumption from those cases. See 521 U.S., at 220–221 (Shared Time program at issue in *Ball* was "surely invalid . . . [g]iven the holdings in *Meek* and *Wolman*" regarding instructional materials and equipment). Today we simply acknowledge what has long been evident and was evident to the Ninth and Fifth Circuits and to the District Court.

The judgment of the Fifth Circuit is reversed.

Glossary

Bill of Rights—the first ten Amendments to the U.S. Constitution, encompassing basic personal freedoms and limits on government interference with those rights

Codify—create a statute to reflect a policy or court decision, thus placing the law within a set of statutes, or "code"

Corporal punishment—discipline involving physical force, such as paddling

De minimis—describes relatively inconsequential infractions that do not require judicial scrutiny

Curing—The process of modifying a document or practice to conform to legal requirements

Due process—the procedures required in a given situation to avoid erroneous deprivation of personal rights (i.e., life, liberty, property) guaranteed by the Fourteenth Amendment

Eighth Amendment—the provision in the Bill of Rights that guarantees, in criminal law alone, the right of individuals to be free of "excessive bail," "excessive fines," and "cruel and unusual punishment" (*see* corporal punishment)

Establishment Clause—the constitutional prohibition against governmental promotion of a particular faith or of religion over nonbelief

First Amendment—the first provision of the Bill of Rights, which includes the rights to freedom of religion, speech, press, assembly, and association, and to demand government action

Fourth Amendment—the provision in the Bill of Rights that guarantees, under certain circumstances, the right of individuals to be free of warrantless searches

Free Exercise Clause—that part of the First Amendment that guarantees freedom of religious practice

Free Speech Clause—that part of the First Amendment that guarantees "freedom of speech," which has been interpreted to mean free expression in any medium, though the freedom is not absolute, especially in the context of public school student speech

Lemon test—a three-pronged method of Establishment Clause analysis, now out of favor, that attempts to discern constitutional behavior according to the practice's purpose, process, and result (*see* neutrality)

Liberty interest—the Fourteenth Amendment principle that people, including public school students, have a right to personal discretion that cannot be limited by government without a formal process to justify the restriction

Limited open forum—a First Amendment situation in which a school is open to outside organizations and/or points of view, thus, under the Free Speech Clause, barring the public school or district from creating a limited public forum that discriminates against participation by other organizations or points of view on the basis of the content of the message

Neutrality—the currently prevailing concept in Establishment Clause jurisprudence that requires that government neither favor nor disfavor religious practice in policies and practices

Notice and hearing—the constitutionally protected procedural rights of a public school student facing suspension for ten or more days to know the infraction with which he or she is charged and to be able to give testimony about the circumstances giving rise to the charge; the limited procedure does not include typical rights of criminal defendants to trial by jury and so on

Overrule—to negate a prior ruling or request; in the case of the U.S. Supreme Court, to reverse a prior holding

Plurality opinion—when no majority opinion is issued by the U.S. Supreme Court, the opinion of the largest group of justices (at least two but fewer than five) prevailing in a particular case

Probable cause—the standard for a search of a person by a government when criminal wrongdoing is suspected (*see* reasonable cause; search and seizure)

Progeny—decisions in later cases that rely on the reasoning from an earlier judicial opinion

Property interest—the Fourteenth Amendment principle that people, including public school students, have a right to their legitimately gained property that cannot be limited by government without a formal process to justify the restriction; the right to a public education is a recognized property interest giving rise, in some circumstances, to the need for formal suspension procedures (*see* notice and hearing)

Reasonable cause—the justification for public school officials to search students when there is merely a reasonable expectation of finding contraband; a lower standard than probable cause (*see* probable cause; search and seizure)

Search and seizure—a government's limited right to search people and their belongings on the basis of cause (*see* probable cause; reasonable cause)

State action—government practice at any level

CHAPTER THREE

School District Issues

Curriculum

In the United States, curriculum is almost always a discretionary matter for educators to decide within usually broad parameters set by state education departments under legislative direction. The courts give wide latitude to curricular decisions, seeking to distance themselves from micromanaging what is or is not taught. See, for example, *Hazelwood School Dist. v. Kuhlmeier,* 484 U.S. 260 (1988) (contents of student newspaper subject to legitimate curricular and pedagogical judgment of principal); *Board of Education, Island Trees Union Free School District No. 26 v. Pico,* 457 U.S. 853 (1982), infra (content of classroom libraries subject to broad discretion as curricular in nature); *Virgil v. School Bd. of Columbia County,* 862 F.2d 1917 (11th Cir. 1989) (refusing to overturn board decision to remove "inappropriate" material from the curriculum); *Mozert v. Hawkins County Public Schools,* 827 F.2d 1058 (6th Cir. 1987), cert. denied, 484 U.S. 1066 (1988) (refusing to allow child to "opt out" of core curriculum reading course); *Smith v. Board of School*

Comm. of Mobile, 827 F.2d 684 (11th Cir. 1987) (refusing to require school board to remove books from curriculum that are offensive to parents' religious beliefs). According to the National School Boards Association (www.nsba.org), "Courts are traditionally reluctant to wade into educational decisions, especially on issues such as curriculum. Judges prefer to leave these matters to the experts: school boards and administrators. But they will intervene to protect the legal rights of students and parents."

Hazelwood School District v. Kuhlmeier, 484 U.S. 260 (1988) [some text omitted]

JUSTICE WHITE delivered the opinion of the Court.

This case concerns the extent to which educators may exercise editorial control over the contents of a high school newspaper produced as part of the school's journalism curriculum.

I

Petitioners are the Hazelwood School District in St. Louis County, Missouri; various school officials; Robert Eugene Reynolds, the principal of Hazelwood East High School; and Howard Emerson, a teacher in the school district. Respondents are three former Hazelwood East students who were staff members of Spectrum, the school newspaper. They contend that school officials violated their First Amendment rights by deleting two pages of articles from the May 13, 1983, issue of Spectrum.

Spectrum was written and edited by the Journalism II class at Hazelwood East. The newspaper was published every three weeks or so during the 1982–1983 school year. More than 4,500 copies of the newspaper were distributed during that year to students, school personnel, and members of the community.

The Board of Education allocated funds from its annual budget for the printing of Spectrum. These funds were supplemented by proceeds from sales of the newspaper. The printing expenses during the 1982–1983 school year totaled $4,668.50; revenue from sales was $1,166.84. The other costs associated with the newspaper—such as supplies, textbooks, and a portion of the journalism teacher's salary—were borne entirely by the Board.

The Journalism II course was taught by Robert Stergos for most of the 1982–1983 academic year. Stergos left Hazelwood East to take a job in private industry on April 29, 1983, when the May 13 edition of Spectrum was nearing completion, and petitioner Emerson took his place as newspaper adviser for the remaining weeks of the term.

The practice at Hazelwood East during the spring 1983 semester was for the journalism teacher to submit page proofs of each Spectrum issue to Principal Reynolds for his review prior to publication. On May 10, Emerson delivered the proofs of the May 13 edition to Reynolds, who objected to two of the articles scheduled to appear in that edition. One of the stories described three Hazelwood East students' experiences with pregnancy; the other discussed the impact of divorce on students at the school.

Reynolds was concerned that, although the pregnancy story used false names "to keep the identity of these girls a secret," the pregnant students still might be identifiable from the text. He also believed that the article's references to sexual activity and birth control were inappropriate for some of the younger students at the school. In addition, Reynolds was concerned that a student identified by name in the divorce story had complained that her father "wasn't spending enough time with my mom, my sister and I" prior to the divorce, "was always out of town on business or out late playing cards with the guys," and "always argued about everything" with her mother. Reynolds believed that the student's parents should have been given an opportunity to respond to these remarks, or to consent to their publication. He was unaware that Emerson had deleted the student's name from the final version of the article.

Reynolds believed that there was no time to make the necessary changes in the stories before the scheduled press run, and that the newspaper would not appear before the end of the school year if printing were delayed to any significant extent. He concluded that his only options under the circumstances were to publish a four-page newspaper instead of the planned six-page newspaper, eliminating the two pages on which the offending stories appeared, or to publish no newspaper at all. Accordingly, he directed Emerson to withhold from publication the two pages containing the stories on pregnancy and divorce. He informed his superiors of the decision, and they concurred.

Respondents subsequently commenced this action in the United States District Court for the Eastern District of Missouri, seeking a declaration that their First Amendment rights had been violated, injunctive relief, and monetary damages. After a bench trial, the District Court denied an injunction, holding that no First Amendment violation had occurred.

II

Students in the public schools do not "shed their constitutional rights to freedom of speech or expression at the schoolhouse gate." *Tinker, supra,* at 506. They cannot be punished merely for expressing their personal views on the school premises—whether "in the cafeteria, or on the playing field, or on the campus during the authorized hours,"—unless school authorities have reason to believe that such expression will "substantially interfere with the work of the school or impinge upon the rights of other students."

We have nonetheless recognized that the First Amendment rights of students in the public schools "are not automatically coextensive with the rights of adults in other settings," *Bethel School District No. 403 v. Fraser,* 478 U.S. 675, 682 (1986), and must be "applied in light of the special characteristics of the school environment." *Tinker, supra,* at 506; *cf. New Jersey v. T.L.O.,* 469 U.S. 325, 341–343 (1985). A school need not tolerate student speech that is inconsistent with its "basic educational mission," *Fraser, supra,* at 685, even though the government could not censor similar speech outside the school. Accordingly, we held in *Fraser* that a student could be disciplined for having delivered a speech that was "sexually explicit" but not legally obscene at an official school assembly, because the school was entitled to "disassociate itself " from the speech in a manner that would demonstrate to others that such vulgarity is "wholly inconsistent with the 'fundamental values' of public school education." 478 U.S. at 685–686. We thus recognized that "[t]he determination of what manner of speech in the classroom or in school assembly is inappropriate properly rests with the school board," *id.* at 683, rather than with the federal courts. It is in this context that respondents' First Amendment claims must be considered.

A

We deal first with the question whether Spectrum may appropriately be characterized as a forum for public expression. The public schools do not possess all of the attributes of streets, parks, and other traditional public forums that "time out of mind, have been used for purposes of assembly, communicating thoughts between citizens, and discussing public questions." Hence, school facilities may be deemed to be public forums only if school authorities have "by policy or by practice" opened those facilities "for indiscriminate use by the general public," *Perry Education Assn. v. Perry Local Educators' Assn.,* 460 U.S. 37, 47 (1983), or by some segment of the public, such as student organizations. If the facilities have instead been reserved for other intended purposes, "communicative or otherwise," then no public forum has been created, and school officials may impose reasonable restrictions on the speech of students, teachers, and other members of the school community.

The policy of school officials toward Spectrum was reflected in Hazelwood School Board Policy 348.51 and the Hazelwood East Curriculum Guide. Board Policy 348.51 provided that

> [s]chool sponsored publications are developed within the adopted curriculum and its educational implications in regular classroom activities.

The Hazelwood East Curriculum Guide described the Journalism II course as a "laboratory situation in which the students publish the school newspaper applying skills they have learned in Journalism I." The lessons that were to be learned from the Journalism II course, according to the Curriculum Guide, included development of journalistic skills under deadline pressure, "the legal, moral, and ethical restrictions imposed upon journalists within the school community," and "responsibility and acceptance of criticism for articles of opinion." *Ibid.* Journalism II was taught by a faculty member during regular class hours. Students received grades and academic credit for their performance in the course.

School officials did not deviate in practice from their policy that production of Spectrum was to be part of the educational curriculum, and a "regular classroom activit[y]." The District Court found that Robert Stergos, the journalism teacher during most of the 1982–1983 school year, "both had the authority to exercise, and in fact exercised, a great deal of control over Spectrum." For example, Stergos selected the editors of the newspaper, scheduled publication dates, decided the number of pages for each issue, assigned story ideas to class members, advised students on the development of their stories, reviewed the use of quotations, edited stories, selected and edited the letters to the editor, and dealt with the printing company. Many of these decisions were made without consultation with the Journalism II students. The District Court thus found it

> clear that Mr. Stergos was the final authority with respect to almost every aspect of the production and publication of Spectrum, including its content.

Moreover, after each Spectrum issue had been finally approved by Stergos or his successor, the issue still had to be reviewed by Principal Reynolds prior to publication. Respondents' assertion that they had believed that they could publish "practically anything" in Spectrum was therefore dismissed by the District Court as simply "not credible." These factual findings are amply supported by the record, and were not rejected as clearly erroneous by the Court of Appeals.

B

The question whether the First Amendment requires a school to tolerate particular student speech—the question that we addressed in *Tinker*—is different from the question whether the First Amendment requires a school affirmatively to promote particular student speech. The former question addresses educators' ability to silence a student's personal expression that happens to occur on the school premises. The latter question concerns educators' authority over school-sponsored publications, theatrical productions, and other expressive activities that students, parents, and members of the public might reasonably perceive to bear the imprimatur of the school. These activities may fairly be characterized as part of the school curriculum, whether or not they occur in a traditional classroom setting, so long as they are supervised by faculty members and designed to impart particular knowledge or skills to student participants and audiences.

Educators are entitled to exercise greater control over this second form of student expression to assure that participants learn whatever lessons the activity is designed to teach, that readers or listeners are not exposed to material that may be inappropriate for their level of maturity, and that the views of the individual speaker are not erroneously attributed to the school. Hence, a school may, in its capacity as publisher of a school newspaper or producer of a school play, "disassociate itself," *Fraser,* 478 U.S. at 685, not only from speech that would "substantially interfere with [its] work . . . or impinge upon the rights of other students," *Tinker,* 393 U.S. at 509, but also from speech that is, for example, ungrammatical, poorly written, inadequately researched, biased or prejudiced, vulgar or profane, or unsuitable for immature audiences. A school must be able to set high standards for the student speech that is disseminated under its auspices—standards that may be higher than those demanded by some newspaper publishers or theatrical producers in the "real" world—and may refuse to disseminate student speech that does not meet those standards. In addition, a school must be able to take into account the emotional maturity of the intended audience in determining whether to disseminate student speech on potentially sensitive topics, which might range from the existence of Santa Claus in an elementary school setting to the particulars of teenage sexual activity in a high school setting. A school must also retain the authority to refuse to sponsor student speech that might reasonably be perceived to advocate drug or alcohol use, irresponsible sex, or conduct otherwise inconsistent with "the shared values of a civilized social order," *Fraser, supra,* at 683, or to associate the school with any position other than neutrality on matters of political controversy. Otherwise, the schools would be unduly constrained from fulfilling their role as

> a principal instrument in awakening the child to cultural values, in preparing him for later professional training, and in helping him to adjust normally to his environment. *Brown v. Board of Education,* 347 U.S. 483, 493 (1954).

Accordingly, we conclude that the standard articulated in *Tinker* for determining when a school may punish student expression need not also be the standard for determining when a school may refuse to lend its name and resources to the dissemination of student expression. Instead, we hold that educators do not offend the First Amendment by exercising editorial control over the style and content of student speech in school-sponsored expressive activities, so long as their actions are reasonably related to legitimate pedagogical concerns.

This standard is consistent with our oft-expressed view that the education of the Nation's youth is primarily the responsibility of parents, teachers, and state and local school officials, and not of federal judges. *See, e.g., Board of Education of Hendrick Hudson Central School Dist. v. Rowley,* 458 U.S. 176, 208 (1982); *Wood v. Strickland,* 420 U.S. 308, 326 (1975); *Epperson v. Arkansas,* 393 U.S. 97, 104 (1968). It is only when the decision to censor a school-sponsored publication, theatrical production, or other vehicle of student expression has no valid educational purpose that the First Amendment is so "directly and sharply implicate[d]," *ibid.,* as to require judicial intervention to protect students' constitutional rights.

III

We also conclude that Principal Reynolds acted reasonably in requiring the deletion from the May 13 issue of Spectrum of the pregnancy article, the divorce article, and the remaining articles that were to appear on the same pages of the newspaper.

The initial paragraph of the pregnancy article declared that "[a]ll names have been changed to keep the identity of these girls a secret." The principal concluded that the students' anonymity was not adequately protected, however, given the other identifying information in the article and the small number of pregnant students at the school. Indeed, a teacher at the school credibly testified that she could positively identify at least one of the girls, and possibly all three. It is likely that many students at Hazelwood East would have been at least as successful in identifying the girls. Reynolds therefore could reasonably have feared that the article violated whatever pledge of anonymity had been given to the pregnant students. In addition, he could reasonably have been concerned that the article was not sufficiently sensitive to the privacy interests of the students' boyfriends and parents, who were discussed in the article but who were given no opportunity to consent to its publication or to offer a response. The article did not contain graphic accounts of sexual activity. The girls did comment in the article, however, concerning their sexual histories and their use or nonuse of birth control. It was not unreasonable for the principal to have concluded that such frank talk was inappropriate in a school-sponsored publication distributed to 14-year-old freshmen and presumably taken home to be read by students' even younger brothers and sisters.

The student who was quoted by name in the version of the divorce article seen by Principal Reynolds made comments sharply critical of her father. The principal could reasonably have concluded that an individual publicly identified as an inattentive parent—indeed, as one who chose "playing cards with the guys" over home and family—was entitled to an opportunity to defend himself as a matter of journalistic fairness. These concerns were shared by both of Spectrum's faculty advisers for the 1982–1983 school year, who testified that they would not have allowed the article to be printed without deletion of the student's name.

Principal Reynolds testified credibly at trial that, at the time that he reviewed the proofs of the May 13 issue during an extended telephone conversation with Emerson, he believed that there was no time to make any changes in the articles, and that the newspaper had to be printed immediately or not at all. It is true that Reynolds did not verify whether the necessary modifications could still have been made in the articles, and that Emerson did not volunteer the information that printing could be delayed until the changes were made. We nonetheless agree with the District Court that the decision to excise the two pages containing the problematic articles was reasonable, given the particular circumstances of this case. These circumstances included the very recent replacement of Stergos by Emerson, who may not have been entirely familiar with Spectrum editorial and production procedures, and the pressure felt by Reynolds to make an immediate decision so that students would not be deprived of the newspaper altogether.

In sum, we cannot reject as unreasonable Principal Reynolds' conclusion that neither the pregnancy article nor the divorce article was suitable for publication in Spectrum. Reynolds could reasonably have concluded that the students who had written and edited these articles had not sufficiently mastered those portions of the Journalism II curriculum that pertained to the treatment of controversial issues and personal attacks, the need to protect the privacy of individuals whose most intimate concerns are to be revealed in the newspaper, and "the legal, moral, and ethical restrictions imposed upon journalists within [a] school community" that includes adolescent subjects and readers. Finally, we conclude that the principal's decision to delete two pages of Spectrum, rather than to delete only the offending articles or to require that they be modified, was reasonable under the circumstances as he understood them. Accordingly, no violation of First Amendment rights occurred.

The judgment of the Court of Appeals for the Eighth Circuit is therefore *reversed.*

While states have ultimate authority in setting curricula—even for private and home schools under their sweeping regulatory powers—and the federal government is now involved through the testing provisions of the No Child Left Behind Act (see chapter four), most day-to-day decisions about instructional content are made by school boards and educators at the district, school, and classroom levels. Parents and students have little say, except insofar as they can convince politicians or educators to tailor lessons to accommodate their suggestions.

Regarding regulation of private school and home school curricula, states usually forbear from prescribing curricula, except to require equivalence with public school instruction in secular subjects. Partly this is a political decision, in deference to the considerable electoral strength of parents, religious groups, and others committed to preserving a vigorous system of private education as an alternative to public schools. But this political decision is supported by early education case law in which the Supreme Court forbade states from prohibiting private schooling (*Pierce v. Society of Sisters,* 268 U.S. 510 (1925)) and unduly interfering with private school curricula favored by parents in those schools (*Meyer v. Nebraska,* 262 U.S. 390 (1923)).

Facts

Jehovah's Witnesses make an offer to a public school district to provide elementary, middle, and high school libraries with publications that encourage religious devotion, such as *Awake* magazines and a paperback book, *Questions Young People Ask—Answers That Work,* described as having 39 chapters and 320 pages that "answer many questions, such as: How can I cope with peer pressure? Should I quit school? How can I say no to premarital sex? Why say no to drugs?"

Find

An example of the manner in which most curricula are adopted comes from the mandated policy of the Dubuque, Iowa, public schools:

> Curriculum development shall be an ongoing process in the Dubuque Community School District. Each curriculum area shall be reviewed, and revised when necessary, according to the timelines set out by the superintendent. These timelines will provide for review of each curriculum area on a regular cycle.
>
> The superintendent shall be responsible for curriculum development and for determining the most effective way for conducting research of the school district's curriculum needs and a long-range curriculum development program.
>
> In making recommendations to the Board, the superintendent shall propose a curriculum that will:
>
> - fulfill the philosophy of the school district;
> - incorporate data/information from the needs assessment for student learning conducted by curriculum design teams;
> - directly correlates with established content standards and benchmarks;
> - be based upon sound educational research;

- articulate courses of study from kindergarten through grade twelve;
- identify instructional objectives for each course and, at the elementary level, for each grade;
- allow schools flexibility in identifying the means by which instructional objectives are met while providing for systematic evaluation of the procedures and methods for attaining the objectives;
- provide for effective monitoring of a student's progress;
- provide for the needs of all students regardless of their program of study; and
- include, if feasible, the course offerings requested by the students, parents, and community members

The superintendent shall be responsible for curriculum implementation and for determining the most effective way of providing organized assistance and monitoring the level of implementation.

Regular evaluation of the curriculum will be conducted to ensure that the written and delivered curriculum is having the desired effect for students. The superintendent shall be responsible for curriculum evaluation and for determining the most effective way of ensuring that assessment activities are integrated into instructional practices as part of school improvement.

As part of this evaluation process, student assessment information will be used to determine long-range and annual improvement goals. These goals will be reported in the district improvement plan and in the annual progress report to the community and the Iowa Department of Education.

It shall be the responsibility of the superintendent to keep the Board apprised of necessary curriculum changes and revisions and to develop administrative regulations for curriculum development and recommendations to the Board.

Adopted: August 14, 1989
Revised: January 8, 2001

In *Board of Education, Island Trees Union Free School District No. 26 v. Pico,* 457 U.S. 853 (1982), discussed at greater length below, the Supreme Court drew a line between classroom libraries, which it deemed curricular and thus subject to great deference by the Court, and school libraries, which it stated came within the **ambit** of judicial scrutiny regard-

Ambit
scope; breadth

ing the collection's political content so that a reasonably open **marketplace of ideas** could be assured while allowing for discretion on the basis of educators' professional expertise in areas of age appropriateness, literary quality, and relevance to student interests.

Marketplace of ideas the ideal of freely exchanged thoughts and opinions protected by the First Amendment

Perhaps since school libraries are subject to greater judicial scrutiny than curricular classroom libraries, school librarians should be especially careful in deciding on whether to add *Awake* and *Questions Young People Ask* to their collections, although here we are dealing with a question regarding the materials' inclusion, rather than exclusion as in *Pico.* One consideration might be that while the Jehovah's Witness materials clearly promote the Jehovah's Witnesses' faith and are not secular publications that either objectively explain the religion or place it in a comparative religious context, they might legitimately be used as reference materials. Are the magazines and books different from holy texts such as the Bible or Koran, which have demonstrable roles as primary source material in teaching about Judaism, Christianity, and Islam? Finally, if the Jehovah's Witness materials are included in the library collection, does that trigger an automatic right for other religious groups (be they traditional or nontraditional) to have their tracts included too?

Quasi-judicial bodies an administrative body that acts in a judicial manner, rendering decisions on disagreements between two parties, but that is part of the executive branch rather than the judiciary

Arbitrary and capricious the dual standard applied by courts to determine whether an administrative decision is illegal; opposite of the "rational basis" standard

Rational basis the standard courts use to determine whether an administrative determination should be upheld; opposite of impermissible "arbitrary and capricious" determinations

Before we reach the Establishment Clause issues, an examination of basic district rules about library accessions is worthwhile. The need for such written, properly approved documents cannot be overemphasized. Without such paraphernalia—so loathed by just about everybody as bureaucratic mumbo jumbo—courts or **quasi-judicial bodies** such as administrative tribunals (see chapter one) will have little basis for favorable review of a district's decision. As a result, otherwise commonsense judgments about curricular material will appear to be **arbitrary and capricious**, rather than having a **rational basis** , and are likely to be struck down.

As an example, the library accessions policy of the York, Maine, public schools includes an

"Instructional and Library Materials Selection" policy and a "Request for Reconsideration of Materials" appeal form:

Instructional and Library Materials Selection

Objectives of Selection

The York School Committee recognizes that it is the primary objective of the library media centers and the instructional program in our schools to implement, enrich, and support the education programs of the schools. It is the duty of the library media centers and the instructional program to provide a wide range of materials on all levels of difficulty, with diversity of appeal and the presentation of different points of view.

To this end, the School Committee asserts that the responsibility of the School Library Media Centers and the instructional program is:

A. To provide materials that will enrich and support the curriculum, taking into consideration the varied interests, abilities, and maturity levels of the students served;
B. To provide materials that will stimulate growth in factual knowledge, literacy appreciation, aesthetic values and ethical standards;
C. To provide a background of information which will enable students to make intelligent judgments in their daily lives;
D. To provide materials on opposing sides of public issues so that young citizens may develop under guidance the practice of critical analysis of all media;
E. To provide materials representative of the many religious, ethnic and cultural groups and their contributions to our American heritage; and
F. To place principle above personal opinion and reason above prejudice in selection of materials of the highest quality in order to assure a comprehensive collection appropriate for the users of the library media centers and a variety of resources to be used in the instructional program.

In addition, the School Committee recognizes that the final authority as to the materials to which an individual student will be exposed rests with the student's parents or guardians. However, at no time will the wishes of one child's parents to restrict his/her reading or viewing of a particular item infringe on other parents' rights to permit their children to read or view the same material.

Responsibility for Selection of Instructional and Library Materials

The School Committee is legally responsible for all matters relating to the operation of the schools. The responsibility for the selection of instructional materials is delegated to the professionally trained personnel employed by the School Committee.

Selection of materials for the library media centers and the instructional program involves many people: principals, teachers, department heads or team leaders, library staff, students, and community members. The responsibility for the coordination of the selections of library and instructional materials and the recommendation for purchase rest with professionally trained personnel. The School Committee is responsible to approve a uniform system of textbooks.

Criteria for Selection

The needs of the individual school, based on knowledge of the curriculum and of the existing collection, are given first consideration.

Materials for purchase are considered on the following bases: overall purpose, timeliness or permanence, importance of the subject matter, quality of the writing-production, readability and popular appeal, authoritativeness, reputation of the publisher–producer, reputation and significance of the author–artist–composer-producer, etc., and the format and price.

Gift materials are judged by the same standards and are accepted or rejected by those standards. Multiple copies of outstanding and much-in-demand materials are purchased as needed. Worn or missing standard items are replaced periodically. Out- of-date or no-longer-useful materials are withdrawn from the collection/circulation. *Procedures for Selection*. In selecting the materials for purchase, the professional personnel evaluate the existing collection, consulting reputable, unbiased, professionally prepared selection aids and specialists from all departments and/or grade levels.

Whenever possible, purchase of non-print materials shall be done only after personal evaluation by the library media specialist and/or other appropriate staff. Reviewing aids may be used in lieu of personal evaluation.

The teachers involved in the use of a particular textbook will be given a role in its selection. In selecting the textbooks for a grade level or area of study, the professional staff involved is authorized to form a textbook selection committee under the supervision of administrative personnel. After a thorough study of textbooks available, the committee will submit recommendations through the principal to the superintendent for review. The Superintendent shall select textbooks, supplies, and materials with the approval of the School Committee and shall make all these purchases under rules adopted by the School Committee.

Students who lose or destroy instructional materials shall be charged a fair value for such replacement.

Challenged Material

Despite the care taken to select materials for student and teacher use and the qualifications of the persons who select the materials, it is recognized that occasional objections may be raised by community members, students, or school staff.

In the event a complaint is made, the following procedures will apply:

A. The complaint shall be heard first by the person providing the materials in question. If a parent has an objection to the required material being used in the classroom for his/her child, that parent may request consideration for alternative materials for his/her child.
B. The complainant shall be referred to the building principal and requested to fill out the "Request for Reconsideration of Materials" form. A copy of the form will be forwarded to the superintendent.
C. The Superintendent shall appoint a committee composed of the following persons to review the complaint: one principal at the appropriate grade level; one library media specialist; one classroom teacher.
D. The review committee shall: read and examine the materials referred to them; check general acceptance of materials by reading reviews; weigh values and faults against each other and form opinions based on the material as a whole and not on passages or portions pulled out of context; meet to discuss the material and to prepare a written report of it.
E. The Superintendent will make a written decision regarding the status of the material after receipt of the review committee's report, and will inform the complainant of the review committee's recommendations and the decision.

F. No material shall be removed from use until the superintendent has made a final decision.

G. The Superintendent's decision may be appealed to the School Committee. The School Committee may set aside a portion of a regular meeting or call a special meeting for the purpose of receiving information from representatives of the various points of view. The material in question shall be:

1. Reviewed objectively and in its full content;
2. Evaluated in terms of the needs and interest of students, school, curriculum and community;
3. Considered in the light of differing opinions; and
4. Reviewed in light of the criteria for initial selection and purpose as provided herein.

The School Committee will announce its decision in writing.
Legal Reference: TITLE 20A MRSA SEC. 1001 (10-A); 1055 (4); 4002
ME DEPT OF ED RULE CHAP. 125.22

Adopted by School Committee: 4/24/02

NEPN/NSBA Code: IJJ-E1 YORK SCHOOL DEPARTMENT
Request for Reconsideration of Materials

The York School Committee has delegated the responsibility for selection and evaluation of instructional materials to the professionally trained personnel whom it employs, and has established reconsideration procedures to address concerns about those resources. If you wish to request reconsideration of instructional or library resources, please return the completed form to the Coordinator of Library/Media Services, York School Dept., 30 Organug Rd., York, ME 03909.

Request initiated by ______________________________
Date ______________ Telephone ___________________
Address ____
City________________________ Zip Code ___________

Do you represent: ________ Self ________ Organization (specify)
Other group (specify) ______________________________

Resource on which you are commenting: _______________
____ Book ___ Textbook ___ Video __ Audio recording ___ Display

___ Magazine ___ Newspaper ___ Other (please specify): ___

Title ___

Author/Producer ___

What brought this resource to your attention? ___

Have you examined the entire resource? ___

What concerns you about the resource? (use additional pages if needed) ___

What action do you feel the School Department should take?

___

Are there resource(s) you suggest to provide additional information and/or other viewpoints on this topic? ___

A methodical review of how the Jehovah's Witness materials might be treated under this policy and appeals process is beyond the scope of this brief primer, but several matters deserve emphasis.

First are the legal foundations for any enforceable policy. The "Instructional and Library Materials Selection" policy is explicitly based on state statutory and regulatory authority, in this case identified in the penultimate section of the document. Also noted is the date the policy was approved by the York School Committee. Should any question arise as to the policy's validity, a quick look at the School Committee's minutes for that date will suffice.

Another matter of great significance is that the policy delegates discretion in the choice of instructional materials to educators. While the School Committee and even the State of Maine could dictate curricular material, the policy reflects the general thrust of American public education law, discussed above, to leave those decisions to educators first, localities next, then states, and never the federal government. While this clear statement may wobble in the context of No Child Left Behind, with its federal requirements for student achievement and research-based methods, the principle remains, and the ability of educators to make rationally based curriculum and instructional decisions, within the scope of discretion left to them by state and local governments, remains a legal touchstone.

The ability of a school board to divest itself of certain controversial material was addressed by the Supreme Court in *Pico*. The Court held that if it could be proven that the nine banned books, such as *Best Short Stories of Negro Writers* edited by Langston Hughes and *Slaughterhouse-Five* by Kurt Vonnegut Jr., were removed from the district's school libraries because, as the school board stated, they were "anti-American, anti-Christian, anti-Semitic, and just plain filthy," then the school board had violated the First Amendment by unconstitutionally proscribing speech.

Similarly, schools boards may not cross another First Amendment line: the Establishment Clause. When the school board in Dover, Pennsylvania, voted that the concept of "intelligent design" was to be taught in district science classes alongside lessons on evolution, the policy was challenged in *Kitzmiller v. Dover Area School District,* 400 F.Supp.2d 707 (M.D. Pa. 2005). Holding for plaintiffs, the Federal District Court for the Middle District of Pennsylvania determined that intelligent design was essentially a religious belief and its teaching in science classrooms was an impermissible state endorsement of religious faith. Judge Jones' 139-page opinion is notable for its breadth in the area of the limits on school districts to impose curricular requirements and is a rare instance of a District Court decision having important precedential effect, in part because the *Kitzmiller* board was defeated in its next election, so that no appeal was taken up and the policy was officially **repealed.**

Repeal
to withdraw a statute or regulation by official action

Regarding other Establishment Clause issues that arise from these facts, if a librarian wants to shelve the materials, he or she should justify the decision solely on the basis of library policy: secular utility, age appropriateness, relation to the curriculum, and the like. And if such items are included in the collection, similar items from other religions need not be added, though objective reasons not based on the particular religious content of the works would have to be made clear. Of course, a librarian might make the opposite choice and still stay within the law, as long as that choice, too, met the objective criterion of reasonableness and was not based on favoritism or antagonism toward the materials' religious content.

Teacher Discipline

Facts

A 28-year veteran art teacher took 89 fifth graders from an upscale suburban community to an urban art museum. The visit had been approved by the principal, and the teacher toured the museum in planning the visit. The class was accompanied by four other teachers, approximately a dozen parents, and a museum guide. While viewing the galleries, the students saw nude artwork. A parent complaint about exposing students to "nude statues and other nude art representations" triggered a principal's letter to the teacher's file and disciplinary proceedings, including denial of transfer to another school in the district, nonrenewal of the teacher's contract, and suspension with pay. The charges cited the teacher's insufficient display of student artwork, wearing flip-flops against school rules, poor use of time during the trip, and other lesson planning issues. No prior negative evaluations were in the teacher's file. As a result of the charges, the teacher complained to the school board, eventually settling for the balance of her annual salary, inclusion of a prior letter of recommendation in her file, and prohibition against her taking future related legal action.

Find

Grievance machinery
the procedures required when a teacher alleges a breach of contract by a school official, as when disciplinary charges are brought against the teacher

Tenure
the right to automatic contract renewal

Academic freedom
the general ability of educators to teach and assign material free from political intimidation

Disciplinary action against teachers and other school employees usually rests squarely upon the facts of the case and contractually negotiated procedures for ascertaining the facts and punishment, if any. That is why, under the facts above, the teacher engaged the **grievance machinery** of the district rather than immediate court-based litigation under the Fourteenth Amendment's Due Process Clause, the First Amendment's Free Speech Clause, or state claims. Representation could be obtained through union counsel or individually, depending on the circumstances and union policies.

State statutory guarantees of **tenure** and other procedural safeguards may exist. In addition, constitutional protections may arise where public school teachers' freedom of expression or other rights are implicated. After a long struggle with the idea of **academic freedom,** the Supreme Court finally ruled in *Keyishian v. Board of Regents,* 385 U.S. 589 (1967), that publicly employed teachers are entitled to free speech and political privacy rights under the First Amendment. The case involved "loyalty oaths" and prohibitions against "treasonable and seditious speech" required of teachers and professors in New York State. *Keyishian* held that "academic freedom . . . is a special concern of the First Amendment, which does not tolerate laws that cast a pall of orthodoxy over the classroom."

In *Pickering v. Board of Education,* 391 U.S. 563 (1968), the Supreme Court found that the Constitution prohibits a public school district from dismissing a teacher for writing a letter to the editor of a local newspaper criticizing the school board's allocation of school funds between educational and athletic programs and the district's strategy for informing the public why additional tax revenues were being sought for the schools. The Court held that the issue was a matter of general public attention and could not be presumed to have interfered with the teacher's performance or the school's general operation. The teacher's public statements were therefore entitled to the same protection as if they had been made by a member of the general public, and, without proof that even false statements in the letter were knowingly or recklessly made, did not justify the board in dismissing the teacher from public employment.

A later case, *Mt. Healthy City Board of Education v. Doyle,* 429 U.S. 274 (1977), casts *Pickering* in a more limited light. In *Mt. Healthy,* an untenured teacher was denied renewal of his contract after he leaked a principal's memorandum regarding teachers' dress and appearance to a local radio station, which aired the story in its news broadcast. The teacher, who was a leader of the district's union chapter, had previously been involved in several incidents in which he had had an altercation with another teacher, had had an argument with school cafeteria employees, had sworn at students, and had made obscene gestures to female students. Doyle challenged the nonrenewal under *Pickering,* charging that his bringing the dress code memorandum to public attention was protected under the First and Fourteenth Amendments to the Constitution. However, the Supreme Court unanimously held that the Board of Education was constitutionally permitted to terminate the teacher, though his protected activities played a substantial part in their decision, if the employee's other actions provided an independent basis for termination.

Further complicating the analysis is *Garcetti v. Ceballos,* 547 U.S. — (2006), in which the Court held that statements by public employees made in the context of their employment are not protected under the First Amendment. Ceballos, a Los Angeles County deputy district attorney, had written an internal memorandum critical of a decision by his superiors for which he was subsequently disciplined. A 5–4 majority of the Supreme Court determined that such speech, made in the context of public employment rather than as a private citizen as in *Pickering,* is not subject to First Amendment protection.

Prior decisions in the context of public education make tenure status a determining factor in teachers' free speech rights. *Perry v. Sindermann,* 408 U.S. 593 (1972), held that a nontenured state college professor and union activist was entitled to notice and hearing regarding his termination for allegedly protected speech because of an expectation of tenure under the college's policy of **de facto tenure.** But a nontenured state college professor was found to have no Fourteenth Amendment due process right to notice and hearing when, without any stated reason, his contract was not renewed. Despite evidence he had engaged in protected speech against the college, the Court held that no constitutional liberty or property interest had been involved since there was no policy creating an expectation of tenure (*Board of Regents v. Roth,* 408 U.S. 564 (1972)).

De facto tenure
a system in which tenure is automatic and thus expected on the basis of teacher seniority

Though untenured, the teacher in the art museum case clearly had a right to a hearing under her contract with the school district. She also had a right to escort her students to the museum according to the school's trip policies, without needing to invoke the broader rights of academic freedom under *Keyishian.* But *Pickering* is probably unhelpful since she made no statement of general public interest concerning the place of nudity in students' art education and, even if this might be tacitly understood, the *Garcetti* case might undercut a claim of protected speech since her action was performed in the context of her employment.

Even if the district's other claimed bases for dismissal were **pretextual,** as seems likely, and the main reason for termination was the students' exposure to arguably offensive art (though offense, taken alone, is rarely a legitimate cause for disciplinary action), the case probably comes down to whether the teacher violated district regulations, rather than an argument over academic freedom. In this, however, she seems to have a strong claim of legitimate

Pretextual
Describes a legally permissible reason put forth in place of the actual reason for an action, which may be illegal

activities, approved by the principal, and the district's decision to settle rather than litigate was probably wise.

Facts

A public elementary school principal was told by a parent that a nine-year-old had told another child that she was having sex with an adult. The mother of the nine-year-old reported to school personnel that her child was sad and was "acting differently at home." Rather than immediately reporting the incident to child welfare authorities, the principal investigated the allegations. For this, the principal was arrested and charged with failure to report suspected child abuse under the state's child abuse reporting statute.

Find

In today's highly regulated educational environment, a plethora of mandated tripwires await school employees. Even the most cautious educator can become ensnared in this hodge-podge of federal, state, and local requirements arising from constitutional, statutory, regulatory, contractual, judicial, and administrative sources. Indeed, in this case, the principal's caution was her undoing.

All school employees need to know the mandated child abuse reporting requirements for their locality. Every state has enacted its own legislation based on the federal **Child Abuse Prevention and Treatment Act (CAPTA)**, 42 U.S.C. 5101, et seq., as frequently amended since it was first enacted in 1974.

Child Abuse Prevention and Treatment Act (CAPTA)
the main source of federal and state authority to regulate child abuse reporting by educators and other professionals

If the district doesn't provide it, the employee should take the initiative and draw up a numbered list of steps, with contact information, clearly stating whom to call and when if suspicion of abuse occurs. Written record-keeping is also important—sometimes special forms are mandated by the district—so that any investigation of reporting or non-reporting can be immediately addressed.

A typical source of law for this type of incident is a district policy, based on state law, that sets forth required behavior when information about alleged child abuse comes to employees' attention. Los Angeles' requirements follow:

Child Abuse Reporting Information Sheet

Los Angeles Unified School District ("District") would like to take this opportunity to apprise you of some of its significant policies and procedures regarding the reporting of child abuse or neglect to child protective agencies. The purpose of this summary is to serve as a quick reference guide to those policies and procedures, which are pertinent to the detection and reporting of child abuse or neglect. In addition to this summary, the District *strongly recommends that you familiarize yourself with the District's Child Abuse Reporting Bulletin, Bulletin No. Z-10 (currently being revised)* [since revised and promulgated as the 26 page Los Angeles Unified School District Policy Bulletin BUL-1347, Nov. 15, 2004]. Please review this summary and the Child Abuse Bulletin carefully as each employee will be expected to adhere to the policies and procedures identified in each of them.

I. California Law

A District employee " . . . in his or her professional capacity or within the scope of his or her employment, has knowledge of or observes a child whom . . . [the employee] knows or reasonably suspects has been the victim of child abuse or neglect . . ." shall report the known or suspected instance of child abuse to a child protective agency immediately, or as soon as practically possible by telephone. Thereafter, the District employee must prepare and send a written report within 36 hours of receiving the information concerning the incident to the child protective agency. (Penal Code Section 11166)

- All District employees are mandated by law to report suspected child abuse. District employees are "mandated reporters." A report made by a mandated reporter is deemed a "mandated report."
- Each District employee is individually responsible for reporting suspected child abuse.
- Reporting suspected child abuse to an employer, supervisor, school principal, school counselor, co-worker, or other person *does not substitute for making a mandated report*

to the appropriate child protective agency.

- Contents of a child abuse report shall remain confidential. Only individuals directly involved in a specific case may have access and/or be privy to information regarding the report and its contents.

II. Definitions

The term "child abuse" is defined to include the following:

- Physical Abuse—actual physical injury.
- Sexual Abuse—sexual assault, sexual exploitation, molestation of child, etc.
- Neglect—negligent failure to provide adequate food, clothing, shelter, medical care or supervision.
- Life Endangerment—any act by person who willfully causes, inflicts or permits any child to endure cruel and inhuman corporal punishment, mental suffering, etc.

III. Child Abuse Reporting Procedures

- If you suspect child abuse or neglect, you must telephone immediately, or as soon as possible, the appropriate child protective agency to report the suspected child abuse.
- Child abuse reports are made to the Department of Children and Family Services ("DFCFCS"), or to the local law enforcement agency.
- A written report must be completed and sent to the child protective agency within 36 hours of receiving the information concerning the incident. The report must be submitted to the agency which received the telephone report.
- The identity of a District employee who reports suspected child abuse shall remain confidential and disclosed only between designated child protective agencies, by court order, or when needed for specified court actions.

IV. Prohibited Actions

- Never contact the child's home or the alleged perpetrator if indicators point to possible abuse or if abuse is suspected prior to making a report.
- Never conduct an investigation of any kind once abuse or neglect is alleged and prior to making a report.
- Never report suspected child abuse or neglect to School Police. *School Police is not deemed a child protective agency.*

V. District Employee Named as Alleged Perpetrator

- District officials may temporarily relocate an employee who has been named as an alleged perpetrator in a report of suspected child abuse.
- A District employee who is temporarily transferred or relocated will not be presumed guilty and will have all appropriate due process rights.

VI. Consequences for Failure to Report

- Generally, District employees are immune from civil and criminal liability when reporting suspected child abuse as required by law.
- Failure to report suspected child abuse is a misdemeanor, and punishable by up to six months in the county jail and/or a $1,000 fine may be imposed.
- A violation of District policies and legal procedures may lead to disciplinary action, up to and including suspension, demotion, and/or termination, from the District.

For further assistance, please contact the office of the general counsel at (213) 241–7600

This type of summary can be very helpful, but reporting requirements often change, as when Los Angeles replaced an earlier policy, Z-10, with a subsequent policy, BUL-1347. Though the district issued this helpfully brief "Child Abuse Reporting Information Sheet" to go along with Z-10, it did not accompany the 26-page revision with a similar digest. Does the earlier summary match the new requirements? Do employees need to master the entirely new BUL-1347 without assistance? Only with hindsight will we know for sure, and then it might be too late.

Practitioners should be aware of the potential problems posed by changing requirements and contact district counsel and their professional associations, including unions, when such changes occur. A reverse burden should be felt by promulgating administrators and professional organizations, who need to support all mandated reporters with current, easy-to-follow instructions. Parents and advocates also need to keep track of the ever-changing policies both to press for compliance and to understand when district employees seem too quick to report mere rumors.

Another problem arises when district procedures appear to conflict with state requirements. Though not present here, a bureaucratic chain of command might require internal reporting of allegations before contacting state child protection officials. And even if district and state procedures are congruent—as in Los Angeles—at what point does a school employee have "reasonable cause to suspect" (or whatever the statutory formulation) that abuse has occurred? Is the third-hand report of an adult to the principal, based on an initial child-to-child conversation, enough to objectively raise a reasonable suspicion of abuse? Does supplementary information about a student's sad mood and "acting differently" make a definitive difference?

In the fact pattern described, the obvious answer—given the principal's arrest—is that even the merest hint of abuse is to be reported and that educators should leave investigation to the professionals. Also, while district channels should be respected, the employee's status as a mandated reporter generally means that his or her obligation is to the state rather than to the local education officials. While district rules need to be clearly understood, student safety and the clear thrust of child protective statutes point in the direction of early reporting rather than tangling with red tape. To lessen any remaining doubt, statutes permit reporters both anonymity and legal immunity, so the price of action is far less than an excess of caution. In the end, the principal was forced to resign and plead to a misdemeanor (to be dismissed after six months "if she does what was asked of her," according to the prosecutor's office), was required to engage in a public education campaign about reporting suspected child abuse, and was rehired by the district as a special education teacher.

To understand the legal burdens on today's principals, it should be added that dissemination of the Child Abuse Reporting Requirements is just one action that principals in the Los Angeles Unified School District were required to certify regarding compliance. Other reporting mandates included, according to Administrator Certification Form 2006–2007, MEM-2558.1:

- **Antibullying Policy (In Schools, at School-Related Events, and Traveling to and from School**), Bulletin No. BUL-1038.1, dated August 16, 2004, issued by the Office of the Chief Operating Officer.
- **Child Abuse and Neglect Reporting Requirements**, Bulletin No. BUL-1347, dated November 15, 2004, issued by the Office of the General Counsel.
- **Order and Distribution of Student Brochures—"Title IX and Nondiscrimination" and "Section 504 and Students with Disabilities,"** Memorandum issued annually by the Office of the General Counsel.
- **Parent Student Handbook Distribution—** Memorandum issued annually by the Office of the Chief Operating Officer.
- **Required Nondiscrimination Notices**—Memorandum issued annually by the Office of the General Counsel. (Reminder to schools and offices to publish and disseminate required nondiscrimination notices.)
- **Responding to and Reporting Hate-Motivated Incidents and Crimes,** Bulletin No. BUL-2047.0, dated October 10, 2005, issued by the Office of the General Counsel.
- **Sexual Harassment Policy (Student-to-Student, Adult-to-Student, and Student-to-Adult),** Bulletin No. BUL-1041, dated May 10, 2004, issued by the Office of the General Counsel.
- **Sexual Harassment Policy—Employees**, Bulletin No. BUL-1893.1, dated August 1, 2005, issued by the Office of the General Counsel.

- **Student and Employee Security**, Bulletin No. BUL-2368.1, dated March 6, 2006, issued by the Office of the Chief Operating Officer.
- **Uniform Complaint Procedures (UCP)**—Memorandum issued annually by the Specially Funded Programs Division. (This memorandum clarifies that uniform complaints may be used to file noncompliance or unlawful discrimination complaints and/or to appeal District decisions regarding such complaints)
- **Update of Safe School Plans Volume 1—(Prevention Programs) and Volume 2 (Emergency Procedures)**—Memorandum issued annually by the Office of Environmental Health and Safety.
- **Title IX Policy/Complaint Procedures**, Bulletin No. BUL-2521.1, dated June 7, 2006, issued by the Office of the General Counsel.

Nobody ever said that being a principal was easy, especially in the area of education law!

Boards of Education and Parent Organizations

Facts

In an effort to encourage parent involvement and greater fundraising, a public school principal endeavors to revive the dormant parent–teacher association (PTA). Finding that no one can locate any previous documentation, the principal asks a group of volunteer parents to help draft a set of bylaws that will help the PTA support the school's strategic plan. The drafting committee gets to work.

Find

This book's emphasis on creating, as well as following, enforceable law (a redundancy) depends on lawmakers following required steps so that mandates they create are not vulnerable to procedural attack. The mundane task of drafting or revising school board, parent association, and other district bylaws—then making sure that they are followed—

is thus critical in ensuring that organizational intentions have the force of law.

Due diligence
a series of investigatory steps consistent with professional requirements

The task of drafting bylaws is usually left to attorneys who cannibalize a version close at hand, perhaps briefly engaging in **due diligence** to ensure consistency with state laws, usually covered in the "not-for-profit" or "nonprofit" corporations section of the statutory code. Perhaps there are even district guidelines or a district model to crib from. Sample bylaws are also available from websites such as the state school boards association or parent–teacher organizations. Tax-exempt status for nonpublic organizations such as PTAs can be obtained by filing Internal Revenue Form 1023, available at www.irs.gov.

But even if well-drafted, bylaws often yellow in the chair's files. From time to time the document is pulled out for reference, only to be rapidly and guiltily re-archived when someone realizes that the board is routinely acting in wholesale violation of its provisions.

This familiar scenario threatens to nullify innumerable board actions and empowers dissidents. Moreover, it squanders the opportunity to align bylaws with the board or PTA's strategic plan, a powerful combination that can strengthen school operations and help to fulfill the school's educational mission. Boards and other school-related organizations should thus periodically engage in the constructive process of bylaw revision to ensure that members are familiar with the document and that it meets current organizational needs.

At a minimum, bylaws need to support the requirements of a working board through boilerplate membership, quorum, and "duties and powers" provisions. Beyond that, a board committee structure is needed to set forth board priorities (a curriculum committee or a public affairs committee?), provisions regarding supervisory and evaluation responsibilities, term limits (fresh blood is often needed), and even a structure for meetings that emphasize accountability for strategic plan deadlines and benchmarks, as well as community involvement.

Connecticut emphasizes school board members' policymaking role, in collaboration with the district superintendent:

Formulation, Adoption, Amendment of Policies

The Board of Education considers policy development its chief function, along with appraisal of the result achieved through its policies. It is through the development and adoption of written policies that the Board shall exercise its leadership in the operation of the school system; it is through study and evaluation of reports concerning the execution of its written policies that the Board shall exercise its control over school operations.

It is the intent of the Board to develop policies and put them in writing so that they serve as guidelines and goals for the successful and efficient functioning of the public schools.

Written policies serve as guides for the discretionary action of those to whom it delegates authority and as a source of information and guidance for all persons who are interested in, and affected by, the district schools.

Changes in needs, conditions, purposes, and objectives will require revisions, deletions, and additions to the policies of present and future Boards. Thus policy development is an ongoing process.

Policy Draft Writer

The Superintendent or designee shall be responsible for recasting Board consensus about policy recommendations into acceptable written form for further deliberation and/or action by the Board.

Attorney Involvement in Policy Development

The Superintendent, as the policy draft writer for the Board, shall seek the advice of counsel when, in the Superintendent's opinion or the Board's, there may be a question of legality or proper legal procedure in the development of a proposed policy.

In the development of policies, the Board will delegate the Superintendent the responsibility of seeking the advice and counsel of appropriate personnel.

The purpose of this provision is that the Board may gain the most complete and reliable information possible on which to base decisions.

Policy Adoption

Adoption of new policies or changing existing policies is solely the responsibility of the Board. Policies will, barring emergencies, be adopted or amended after consideration at two meetings of the Board of Education. The time between Board meetings shall permit further study and also give an opportunity to interested parties to react, however, temporary approval may be granted by the Board in lieu of formal policy to meet emergency conditions or special events which will take place before formal action can be taken.

The agenda and minutes shall be marked to indicate policy matters. The formal adoption of policies shall be by majority vote of present members of the Board of Education and the action shall be recorded in the minutes of the Board of Education. Only those Written statements so adopted and so recorded shall be regarded as official policy.

Policy Dissemination

The Superintendent is directed to establish and maintain an orderly plan for making pertinent policies of the Board known to staff members, students, and others affected by them.

The Superintendent shall arrange to disseminate to staff members all new policies that affect them and their work and shall also provide easy accessibility to an up-to-date policy collection for all employees of the school system and members of the Board.

The Board's policy manual shall be considered a public record and shall be open for inspection at the Board offices.

Reference: Robert's Rules of Order. Revised (Connecticut Association of Boards of Education, 2004)

The process of revising bylaws can prove to be a constructive activity by providing an opportunity to revisit the strategic plan and to build board cohesiveness. The process involves four basic steps, each of which requires the head of the bylaw committee to assume a different role: historian, strategist, politician, and reviewer.

As historian, the first job of the bylaw drafter is to discover what came before. For an established school, this may or may not be easy, since a copy of the current bylaws probably exists somewhere. Once a copy has been unearthed, authenticating the currency of the document may also present a challenge, since bylaws are often not dated, a problem that the re-drafter should make sure is not repeated. Not only should all bylaws be dated by noting their dates of introduction and approval; they should also include a note of the introduction and approval dates of the previous version. This bylaw **legislative history** helps to ensure that the board is using the current version and assures the entire community that it was properly adopted.

Legislative history
the committee reports, testimony, memoranda, floor speeches, and other material leading to legislative enactment, which that may be used to reveal its appropriate interpretation

The historian's job is not finished when the old bylaws are reviewed. Research into bylaws used by other districts or school-based organizations is helpful in uncovering alternative constructions. The variety of board and PTA bylaws is astounding, especially given the widespread use of boilerplate, and a review of how different institutions have sought to solve common problems can be an incalculable source of helpful ideas.

The strategist phase begins after the historian role has produced a thorough, if cursory, review of the extant literature. The strategist is the locked-room part of the process. The principal drafter is alone, thinking. Important source documents are at hand, especially the strategic plan and the current bylaws (or, for a new organization, a sample template), and the drafter needs to figure out how to fit the plan to the bylaws. This phase is extremely important because it will guide the drafter and then the bylaw committee as the process moves into the more public phases of "politician" and "lawyer." But first the drafter must think about what needs to be accomplished through the strategic plan and how those goals can be operationalized through the bylaws' mandated structures and procedures.

For example, it is important to integrate a strong committee structure into board culture. Without the work of committees before plenary sessions, meetings can be a hodgepodge of discussion, reports,

Executive committee
a committee of the board of directors or trustees, usually consisting of board officers, that provides leadership to the board and is given decision-making authority in the full board's absence

Open meetings law
a statute requiring that public business be conducted in public session

Sunshine law
a statute requiring that public business be conducted in public session or that government documents be available for public inspection

non sequiturs, and banter. So bylaws should include an **executive committee** and other such standing and ad hoc committees as may be needed to effectuate the strategic plan and other powers and duties of the board. Thus plenary meetings become accountability sessions where each chair reports on his or her adherence to predetermined deadlines and deliverables.

Following the strategist's role is the politician's. Don't get uppity: drafters and drafting committees are not statesmen, moving respectably through a crowd of docile admirers. They are down-and-dirty pols, agilely attempting to sell a vision even as they accommodate the views of individual board members. So how does the drafting proceed at this stage?

By listening, discussing, and developing consensus! This is a highly interactive process, one in which drafters go back and forth, hearing board member concerns, testing wording, and identifying conflicting ideas and provisions (e.g., number of board members, terms, election procedures, committee roles).

The board chair should take a major leadership role here, subject to **open meetings law** (sometimes called **sunshine law**) constraints, making the document conform to his or her style, as well as meeting individually with other key members (opinion leaders) and anyone else who wants a meeting. This offers an opportunity to form individual relationships that eventually grease passage of the revisions. As important, the process clues the drafting committee into members' pet concerns, which, if they are not in conflict with the overall strategy, can be included in the draft, giving a sense of ownership to those who see their ideas incorporated into the final proposal.

This is not a pristine process. There will be blood on the walls (most of it the drafting committee chair's)! Pieces of the original strategy will have to give way to others' priorities. Drafters need to be agile, collaborative, and perhaps sneaky. For example, drafters can ascribe views to others not in the room, to create the appearance of consensus where none yet exists. But it's all in a good cause: to create a living document that bears fidelity to the strategic plan and that, in the end, all members (or at least the supermajority usually required to pass bylaw amendments) can agree to follow.

Finally, there is a formal role for the reviewer, moving into the whole group arena to hammer out a final draft, satisfy the requirements of state law and tax-exempt status, and engage in the final approval process. The previous roles of historian, strategist, and politician are now put to the test. Did the drafters accurately survey the literature (what if someone comes up with a newly discovered—undated—version of the bylaws)? Was the strategic plan adequately plumbed so that its goals are transparent in the recommended bylaws? Will members see their views reflected in the new draft? Are all statutory, regulatory, and ethical dimensions covered so that the document will stand up to public scrutiny?

This process and these considerations can make the usually mundane task of bylaw revision a genuinely constructive activity, building an effective foundation for district-based and school-based lawmaking.

Race, National Origin, and Gender Discrimination

Equal Protection Clause the constitutional provision in Section 1 of the Fourteenth Amendment that guarantees equal protection on the basis of suspect classifications of race, religion, national origin, and belief, or with respect to fundamental rights such as freedom of speech, the press, and assembly

In the modern era of civil rights law, discrimination complaints generally do not first arise in federal court under the Fourteenth Amendment's **Equal Protection Clause,** which forbids denial by any state (or local government) "to any person within its jurisdiction the equal protection of the laws."

The popular misconception of primary recourse to the courts is reinforced by numerous judicial decisions in the modern era, from *Brown v. Board of Education of Topeka, Kansas,* 347 U.S. 483 (1954) (*Brown I*), to *Parents Involved in Community Schools v. Seattle School District,* 05–908 (U.S. Supreme Court, 2007), and *Meredith v. Jefferson County Board of Education,* 05–915 (U.S. Supreme Court, 2007), covering innumerable fact situations and standards studied by lawyers, educators, and the lay public.

Brown v. Board of Education of Topeka, 347 U.S. 483 (1954) (*Brown I*) [some text omitted]

Mr. Chief Justice Warren delivered the opinion of the Court.

These cases come to us from the States of Kansas, South Carolina, Virginia, and Delaware. They are premised on different facts and different local conditions, but a common legal question justifies their consideration together in this consolidated opinion.

In each of the cases, minors of the Negro race, through their legal representatives, seek the aid of the courts in obtaining admission to the public schools of their community on a nonsegregated basis. In each instance they had been denied admission to schools attended by white children under laws requiring or permitting segregation according to race. This segregation was alleged to deprive the plaintiffs of the equal protection of the laws under the Fourteenth Amendment. In each of the cases other than the Delaware case, a three-judge federal district court denied relief to the plaintiffs on the so-called "separate but equal" doctrine announced by this Court in *Plessy v. Ferguson,* 163 U.S. 537. Under that doctrine, equality of treatment is accorded when the races are provided substantially equal facilities, even though these facilities be separate. In the Delaware case, the Supreme Court of Delaware adhered to that doctrine, but ordered that the plaintiffs be admitted to the white schools because of their superiority to the Negro schools.

The plaintiffs contend that segregated public schools are not "equal" and cannot be made "equal," and that hence they are deprived of the equal protection of the laws. Because of the obvious importance of the question presented, the Court took jurisdiction.

Reargument was largely devoted to the circumstances surrounding the adoption of the Fourteenth Amendment in 1868. It covered exhaustively consideration of the Amendment in Congress, ratification by the states, then-existing practices in racial segregation, and the views of proponents and opponents of the Amendment. This discussion and our own investigation convince us that, although these sources cast some light, it is not enough to resolve the problem with which we are faced. At best, they are inconclusive. The most avid proponents of the post-War Amendments undoubtedly intended them to remove all legal distinctions among "all persons born or naturalized in the United States." Their opponents, just as certainly, were antagonistic to both the letter and the spirit of the Amendments and wished them to have the most limited effect. What others in Congress and the state legislatures had in mind cannot be determined with any degree of certainty.

An additional reason for the inconclusive nature of the Amendment's history with respect to segregated schools is the status of public education at that time. In the South, the movement toward free common schools, supported by general taxation, had not yet taken hold. Education of white children was largely in the hands of private groups. Education of Negroes was almost nonexistent, and practically all of the race were illiterate. In fact, any education of Negroes was forbidden by law in some states. Today, in contrast, many Negroes have achieved outstanding success in the arts and sciences, as well as in the business and professional world. It is true that public school education at the time of the Amendment had advanced further in the North, but the effect of the Amendment on Northern States was generally ignored in the congressional debates. Even in the North, the conditions of public education did not approximate those existing today. The curriculum was usually rudimentary; ungraded schools were common in rural areas; the school term was but three months a year in many states, and compulsory school attendance was virtually unknown. As a consequence, it is not surprising that there should be so little in the history of the Fourteenth Amendment relating to its intended effect on public education.

In approaching this problem, we cannot turn the clock back to 1868, when the Amendment was adopted, or even to 1896, when *Plessy v. Ferguson* was written. We must consider public education in the light of its full development and its present place in American life throughout the Nation. Only in this way can it be determined if segregation in public schools deprives these plaintiffs of the equal protection of the laws.

Today, education is perhaps the most important function of state and local governments. Compulsory school attendance laws and the great expenditures for education both demonstrate our recognition of the importance of education to our democratic society. It is required in the performance of our most basic public responsibilities, even service in the armed forces. It is the very foundation of good citizenship. Today it is a principal instrument in awakening the child to cultural values, in preparing him for later professional training, and in helping him to adjust normally to his environment. In these days, it is doubtful that any child may reasonably be expected to succeed in life if he is denied the opportunity of an education. Such an opportunity, where the state has undertaken to provide it, is a right which must be made available to all on equal terms.

We come then to the question presented: Does segregation of children in public schools solely on the basis of race, even though the physical facilities and other "tangible" factors may be equal, deprive the children of the minority group of equal educational opportunities? We believe that it does.

The effect of this separation on their educational opportunities was well stated by a finding in the Kansas case by a court which nevertheless felt compelled to rule against the Negro plaintiffs: Segregation of white and colored children in public schools has a detrimental effect upon the colored children. The impact is greater when it has the sanction of the law, for the policy of separating the races is usually interpreted as denoting the inferiority of the negro group. A sense of inferiority affects the motivation of a child to learn. Segregation with the sanction of law, therefore, has a tendency to [retard] the educational and mental development of negro children and to deprive them of some of the benefits they would receive in a racial[ly] integrated school system. Whatever may have been the extent of psychological knowledge at the time of *Plessy v. Ferguson,* this finding is amply supported by modern authority. Any language in *Plessy v. Ferguson* contrary to this finding is rejected.

We conclude that, in the field of public education, the doctrine of "separate but equal" has no place. Separate educational facilities are inherently unequal. Therefore, we hold that the plaintiffs and others similarly situated for whom the actions have been brought are, by reason of the segregation complained of, deprived of the equal protection of the laws guaranteed by the Fourteenth Amendment. This disposition makes unnecessary any discussion whether such segregation also violates the Due Process Clause of the Fourteenth Amendment.

Because these are class actions, because of the wide applicability of this decision, and because of the great variety of local conditions, the formulation of decrees in these cases presents problems of considerable complexity. On reargument, the consideration of appropriate relief was necessarily subordinated to the primary question—the constitutionality of segregation in public education. We have now announced that such segregation is a denial of the equal protection of the laws. In order that we may have the full assistance of the parties in formulating decrees, the cases will be restored to the docket, and the parties are requested to present further argument on Questions 4 and 5 previously propounded by the Court for the reargument this Term . The Attorney General of the United States is again invited to participate. The Attorneys General of the states requiring or permitting segregation in public education will also be permitted to appear as *amici curiae* upon request to do so by September 15, 1954, and submission of briefs by October 1, 1954.

11. K.B. Clark, Effect of Prejudice and Discrimination on Personality Development (Mid-century White House Conference on Children and Youth, 1950); Witmer and Kotinsky, Personality in the Making (1952), c. VI; Deutscher and Chein, The Psychological Effects of Enforced Segregation A Survey of Social Science Opinion, 26 J.Psychol. 259 (1948); Chein, What are the Psychological Effects of Segregation Under Conditions of Equal Facilities?, 3 Int. J.Opinion and Attitude Res. 229 (1949); Brameld, Educational Costs, in Discrimination and National Welfare (MacIver, ed., 1949), 44–48; Frazier, The Negro in the United States (1949), 674–681. And see generally Myrdal, An American Dilemma (1944).

Brown v. Board of Education of Topeka, 349 U.S. 294 (1955) (*Brown II*) [some text omitted]

Mr. Chief Justice Warren delivered the opinion of the Court.

These cases were decided on May 17, 1954. The opinions of that date, declaring the fundamental principle that racial discrimination in public education is unconstitutional, are incorporated herein by reference. All provisions of federal, state, or local law requiring or permitting such discrimination must yield to this principle. There remains for consideration the manner in which relief is to be accorded.

Because these cases arose under different local conditions and their disposition will involve a variety of local problems, we requested further argument on the question of relief. In view of the nationwide importance of the decision, we invited the Attorney General of the United States and the Attorneys General of all states requiring or permitting racial discrimination in public education to present their views on that question. The parties, the United States, and the States of Florida, North Carolina, Arkansas, Oklahoma, Maryland, and Texas filed briefs and participated in the oral argument.

These presentations were informative and helpful to the Court in its consideration of the complexities arising from the transition to a system of public education freed of racial discrimination. The presentations also demonstrated that substantial steps to eliminate racial discrimination in public schools have already been taken, not only in some of the communities in which these cases arose, but in some of the states appearing as amici curiae, and in other states as well. Substantial progress has been made in the District of Columbia and in the communities in Kansas and Delaware involved in this litigation. The defendants in the cases coming to us from South Carolina and Virginia are awaiting the decision of this Court concerning relief.

Full implementation of these constitutional principles may require solutions of varied local school problems. School authorities have the primary responsibility for elucidating, assessing, and solving these problems; courts will have to consider whether the action of school authorities constitutes good faith implementation of the governing constitutional principles. Because of their proximity to local conditions and the possible need for further hearings, the courts which originally heard these cases can best perform this judicial appraisal. Accordingly, we believe it appropriate to remand the cases to those courts.

In fashioning and effectuating the decrees, the courts will be guided by equitable principles. Traditionally, equity has been characterized by a practical flexibility in shaping its remedies and by a facility for adjusting and reconciling public and private needs. These cases call for the exercise of these traditional attributes of equity power. At stake is the personal interest of the plaintiffs in admission to public schools as soon as practicable on a nondiscriminatory basis. To effectuate this interest may call for elimination of a variety of obstacles in making the transition to school systems operated in accordance with the constitutional principles set forth in our May 17, 1954, decision. Courts of equity may properly take into account the public interest in the elimination of such obstacles in a systematic and effective manner. But it should go without saying that the vitality of these constitutional principles cannot be allowed to yield simply because of disagreement with them.

While giving weight to these public and private considerations, the courts will require that the defendants make a prompt and reasonable start toward full compliance with our May 17, 1954, ruling. Once such a start has been made, the courts may find that additional time is necessary to carry out the ruling in an effective manner. The burden rests upon the defendants to establish that such time is necessary in the public interest and is consistent with good faith compliance at the earliest practicable date. To that end, the courts may consider problems related to administration, arising from the physical condition of the school plant, the school transportation system, personnel, revision of school districts and attendance areas into compact units to achieve a system of determining admission to the public schools on a nonracial basis, and revision of local laws and regulations which may be necessary in solving the foregoing problems. They will also consider the adequacy of any plans the defendants may propose to meet these problems and to effectuate a transition to a racially nondiscriminatory school system. During this period of transition, the courts will retain jurisdiction of these cases.

The judgments below, except that, in the Delaware case, are accordingly reversed, and the cases are remanded to the District Courts to take such proceedings and enter such orders and decrees consistent with this opinion as are necessary and proper to admit to public schools on a racially nondiscriminatory basis with all deliberate speed the parties to these cases. The judgment in the Delaware case—ordering the immediate admission of the plaintiffs to schools previously attended only by white children—is affirmed on the basis of the principles stated in our May 17, 1954, opinion, but the case is remanded to the Supreme Court of Delaware for such further proceedings as that Court may deem necessary in light of this opinion.

It is so ordered.

Facts

The following documents constitute the origins of a discrimination complaint against the New York City Department of Education by the author, acting as a member of the Citywide Council on High Schools, a parent body organized to advise the Schools Chancellor.

New York City Department of Education
Citywide Council on High Schools

Resolution on New Small High Schools

March 8, 2006

WHEREAS, the Citywide Council on High Schools is an entity created by Chancellor's Regulation D-160 to "advise and comment on educational and instructional policy involving high schools," and

WHEREAS, the Department of Education has opened over 150 new small schools between September 2003 and September 2005 and plans to open many additional small schools and small learning communities in the next three years, and

WHEREAS, the Citywide Council on High Schools has, as a body and among its individual members, conducted fact finding concerning new small high schools, and

WHEREAS, the preliminary data on the previously opened new small schools show that important issues of selection and educational quality remain unresolved; that these schools often create negative impacts of overcrowding, safety, and resource allocation in other schools; and that the Department of Education methodically excludes students with special needs and students with limited English proficiency from these small schools,

BE IT RESOLVED that the Citywide Council on High Schools calls on the Chancellor to substantially delay the implementation of new small high schools until improved planning and implementation can resolve (1) selection processes that do not reflect the aim that small schools target low achieving students, (2) problems of educational quality within new small schools, (3) the negative impact of new small schools on students in other schools, (4) the exclusion of students with special needs and students with limited English proficiency, and

BE IT FURTHER RESOLVED that the Citywide Council on High Schools supports issuing a letter of complaint to federal, State, and local education and law enforcement agencies to investigate illegal discrimination in new schools' admission policies with regard to students with special needs and students with limited English proficiency.

Citywide Council on High Schools
Department of Education of the City of New York

Citywide Council on High Schools
Department of Education of the City of New York

March 8, 2006

Dear : [per distribution list]

Created by Chancellor's Regulation D-160, the Citywide Council on High Schools advises the New York City Department of Education on high school conditions and policies. At the Council meeting on January 11, 2006, the Chief Executive of the Office of New Schools for the City Department of Education presented an overview of the Chancellor's New Schools Initiative and the "Small Schools" plan for the coming year. According to documents distributed at our meeting, 180 new Small Schools have already opened in the program's first 3 years and an additional 100 have been pledged by the Mayor and Chancellor.

We are writing because, during his remarks, this official stated that the City Department of Education has a deliberate policy to exclude otherwise eligible students with disabilities from the Small Schools, at least during the first 3 years of each school's existence. Implied in these remarks was similar discrimination against students with limited English proficiency. While we understand that not all schools in a district need to be fully inclusive of all special needs and LEP students, this broad, methodical exclusion (documented separately by WNYC reporter Beth Fertig), appears to be a blatant violation of federal, State, and City anti-discrimination and education law. This is especially true in a situation where the Department of Education touts the Small Schools as superior to other existing high schools.

Based on this information, we request an immediate and comprehensive investigation by your office into deliberate, methodical, and purposeful discrimination by the New York City Department of Education's Office of New Schools against students mandated to receive special, bilingual, and ESL education services. We are alerting other federal, State, and City authorities of this matter (list appended) and hope that you can coordinate with them in assuring full legal rights for all students, with such relief as is appropriate to remedy past and prospective discriminatory conduct.

Sincerely,
David C. Bloomfield,
The Citywide Council on High Schools

c: Mr. Richard J. Condon
Special Commissioner of Investigation
for the New York City School District

Ms. Patricia Gatling, Commissioner/Chair
New York City Commission on Human Rights

Hon. Eliot Spitzer
Attorney General of the State of New York

Ms. Rebecca H. Cort
Deputy Commissioner for Vocational and

Educational Services for Individuals with Disabilities
New York State Department of Education

Ms. Stephanie Monroe, Assistant Secretary
Office for Civil Rights
U.S. Department of Education

Mr. Wan J. Kim, Assistant Attorney General
Civil Rights Division
United States Department of Justice

UNITED STATES DEPARTMENT OF EDUCATION
OFFICE FOR CIVIL RIGHTS
32 OLD SLIP, 26TH FLOOR
NEW YORK, NEW YORK 10005

June 7, 2006

RANDOLPH E. WILLS
DIRECTOR
NEW YORK OFFICE
EASTERN DIVISION

David C. Bloomfield, Esq.
The Citywide Council on High Schools
45–18 Court Square, 2nd Floor
Long Island City, New York 11101
Re: Case No. 02–06–1153

Dear Mr. Bloomfield:

The U.S. Department of Education, New York Office for Civil Rights (OCR) previously advised you of its receipt of the above-referenced complaint you filed against the New York City Department of Education (NYCDOE). In telephone conversations with OCR staff members on April 10 and May 24, 2006, and in documentation submitted, you provided additional information regarding your complaint.

You allege that the NYCDOE discriminates on the bases of disability and national origin. Specifically, you allege that the NYCDOE's "New Small Schools Initiative" (the Initiative) discriminates against disabled students requiring self-contained classrooms and students with limited English proficiency (LEP) who require bilingual educational services, by excluding these students from the new small high schools during the first three years of each school's existence. OCR has thoroughly analyzed all of the information provided and has determined that this allegation is appropriate for complaint resolution activities.

OCR is responsible for enforcing Section 504 of the Rehabilitation Act of 1973 (Section 504), as amended, 29 U.S.C. § 794, and its implementing regulation at 34 C.F.R. Part 104, which prohibit discrimination on the basis of disability in programs or activities receiving Federal financial assistance from the U.S. Department of Education. The NYCDOE receives such Federal financial assistance and, therefore, is subject to the provisions of this regulation.

OCR also has jurisdiction as a designated agency under Title II of the Americans with Disabilities Act of 1990 (the ADA), 42 U.S.C. §12131 *et seq.,* and its implementing regulation at 34 C.F.R. Part 35, over complaints alleging discrimination on the basis of disability which are filed against elementary and secondary education systems and institutions, public institutions of higher education and vocational education (other than schools of medicine, dentistry, nursing, and other heath related schools), and public libraries. The NYCDOE is also subject to the provisions of the ADA.

In addition, OCR is responsible for enforcing Title VI of the Civil Rights Act of 1964, 42 U.S.C § 2000d and its implementing regulation at 34 C.F.R. Part 100, which prohibit discrimination on the bases of race, color or national origin in any educational program or activity that receives financial assistance from the U.S. Department of Education. The NYCDOE receives such assistance and, therefore, is subject to the provisions of this regulation.

Please be advised that a U.S. Department of Education regulation prohibits the NYCDOE from harassing or intimidating an individual who has filed a complaint or participated in actions to preserve protected rights. If this should occur, the individual may file a separate complaint alleging such harassment or intimidation.

Please be advised that you may be entitled to file a private suit pursuant to Section 204 of the ADA, regardless of whether or not OCR accepts your complaint for investigation.

Under the Freedom of Information Act, 5 U.S.C. § 552, it may be necessary to release this letter and related correspondence and records upon request. In the event that OCR receives such a request, it will seek to protect, to the extent provided by law, personal information that, if released, could constitute an unwarranted invasion of privacy.

If you have any questions or concerns regarding this matter, please contact xxxxx xxxxxxx, Compliance Team Investigator, at (xxx) xxx-xxxx, or via email at *xxxxxxx@ed.gov,* or xxxxxxxx, or

Compliance Team Attorney, at (xxx) xxx-xxxx or via email at xxxxxxxx@ed.gov.

Sincerely,
/s/

March 17, 2006

Ms. Diane S. Diggs
United States Department of Education
Office for Civil Rights
32 Old Slip, 26th Floor
New York, NY 10005

Re: *Case Number 02–06–1153*

Dear Ms. Diggs:

Thank you for your letter dated March 14, 2006 informing us of receipt of correspondence from the Citywide Council on High Schools and assigning our complaint the above-referenced case number.

Subsequent to mailing our complaint, additional evidence came to light of the City Department of Education's wrongdoing concerning discriminatory conduct toward handicapped and limited English proficient students in the New York City Public Schools. Enclosed, please find an article from the March 14, 2006 issue of the New York "Sun" newspaper, in which an official spokesperson for the New York City Department of Education (City DoE) is quoted as stating, "At the latest, by the third year, [the new small schools] should be able to serve any student that wants to go there." Immediately following, the article explains, "[The spokesperson] said that because new small schools open with only five or six teachers and a limited budget for their first year, they are not often able to offer services for special needs students in their early years."

This seems to us to be an admission of an explicitly discriminatory policy toward a protected class. The Department of Education simply has no right to delay admission of these students to a whole class of schools. Not only are handicapped students disproportionately underrepresented in these schools, but whole groups of handicapped students—those requiring self-contained classrooms—are wholly excluded and required to attend larger, more overcrowded facilities which the City DoE itself believes are inferior to its new small schools.

We would appreciate it if you would add this material to the case file.

Sincerely,
David C. Bloomfield

Office for Civil Rights Consent Form

Office for Civil Rights Consent Form

Please sign, and date section A or section B:

Print your name: *David C. Bloomfield for*
New York Citywide Council on High Schools

Institution named in complaint: *New York City Dept. of Education*

A. I have read the Notice about Investigatory Uses of Personal Information. As a complainant, I understand that in the course of its investigation, OCR may find it necessary to reveal my identity to persons at the institution under investigation. I give my consent. I also understand that under the Freedom of Information Act, OCR may be required to disclose information gathered from me pursuant to this investigation, except in certain instances, such as where disclosure could constitute an unwarranted invasion of my privacy.

/s/ David C. Bloomfield *5/26/06*
(Signature) (Date)

OR

B. I wish to file this complaint, but I do not give my consent for use of personal information. I have read the Notice about Investigatory Uses of Personal Information and I understand that OCR may have to close this complaint if OCR is unable to proceed with an investigation without releasing my identity.

/s/ David C. Bloomfield *5/26/06*
(Signature) (Date)

http://www.ed.gov/about/offices/list/ocr/edlite-consentform.html

Find

The case presented here, portrayed through its initial documentation, describes an important procedural area of education law for both those who allege discrimination and officials who stand accused.

Since at least the mid-1960s, federal, state, and local laws have put the executive branch, rather than the judiciary, at the forefront of civil rights enforcement. Under federal law, this is true for discrimination, as here, on the basis of race, color, or national origin (Title VI of the **Civil Rights Act of 1964,** 42 U.S.C § 2000d, and implementing regulations at 34 C.F.R. Part 100) as well as for discrimination on the basis of gender, including **sexual harassment** (**Title IX of the Education Amendments of 1972** and implementing regulations at 34 C.F.R. Part 106), age (**The Age Discrimination Act of 1975** and implementing regulations at 34 C.F.R. Part 110), and disability (see chapter four; **Section 504 of the Rehabilitation Act of 1973** and implementing regulations at 34 C.F.R. Part 104; Title II of the **Americans with Disabilities Act** and implementing regulations at 28 C.F.R. Part 35; and the Individuals with Disabilities Act and implementing regulations at 34 C.F.R. Parts 300 and 301).

Civil Rights Act of 1964
touchstone civil rights legislation that allowed the federal government to enforce the constitutional right to vote; to protect against discrimination in public accommodations, facilities, and education; to prevent discrimination in federally assisted programs; to extend the Civil Rights Commission; and to establish the Equal Employment Opportunity Commission, among other initiatives to guarantee racial equality within and among the states

Sexual harassment
under Title IX, unwelcome conduct of a sexual nature

Title IX of the Education Amendments of 1972
prohibits discrimination on the basis of gender in federally funded programs

Age Discrimination Act of 1975
prohibits discrimination on the basis of age in federally funded programs

These main statutory and regulatory formulations, and others, are often enacted for only a set period of time before they **sunset,** so are frequently **reauthorized** by Congress with major or minor amendments. Thus, reference to the current version of the law is always of the utmost importance, along with research into relevant, up-to-date case law for the particular jurisdiction in question, since the different federal District Courts and even Circuit Courts are often in conflict with one another in interpreting these complex, changing mandates (see chapter one).

In the case of discrimination in public education, the go-to federal agency is often the **Office of Civil Rights** (**OCR**, see www.ocr.gov/about/offices/list/ocr/), part of the U.S. Department of Education. Under the department's funding authority, which covers every

Americans with Disabilities Act
prohibits discrimination on the basis of disability in employment, state and local government, public accommodations, commercial facilities, transportation, and telecommunications

Sunset
the end of a statute's authorized period of enforceability, requiring reauthorization if the statute is to continue in force

Reauthorize
to reenact a statute after it sunsets

Office of Civil Rights (OCR)
the administrative agency, part of the U.S. Office of Education, empowered to enforce federal civil rights laws in federally funded education programs, including schools and higher education

public school district in the country as well as higher education, OCR conducts investigations and negotiations to secure voluntary compliance and also administrative enforcement proceedings to secure compliance with legislative and regulatory civil rights requirements.

Thus, the Citywide Council on High Schools went first to OCR with its complaint through the informal vehicle of a simple letter, on the basis of an official resolution and a copy of minutes in which an official of the school district stated the existence of an allegedly discriminatory public policy. That was all it took for OCR to then initiate its own investigation, after it "thoroughly analyzed all of the information provided and . . . determined that this allegation is appropriate for complaint resolution activities." Since, usually, the resources of the federal government are far greater than those of a private complainant, requesting assistance from OCR (usually within 180 days of the last alleged act of discrimination) is a robust form of complaint initiation.

As the Citywide Council's letter demonstrates, however, there are other federal, state, and local agencies that can initiate investigations into illegal discrimination, and immediate access to the courts is often an additional possibility, bypassing agency bureaucracies. Depending on the allegations, state or local forums may be the only avenues available for adjudication, since many types of discriminatory conduct, such as those based on sexual orientation, are not protected by federal statute or have different standards for compliance.

Facts

Gay baiting
taunts alleging homosexuality directed at straight or gay students, subject to Title IX enforcement

A heterosexual teenager suffered anti-gay bullying ("**gay baiting**") by classmates from seventh grade until, as a result, he dropped out of high school. He later earned a general equivalency diploma. For four years, students had threatened him, spread homophobic rumors, and called him names such as "bitch," "fag," "faggot," "queer," "flamer," and "masturbator." The victim testified that school officials were aware of the harassment but took insufficient actions to stop it. The school district contended that while it knew of the taunting, students often teased each other using such derisive terms, so it was under no legal responsibility to curtail the children's behavior. The student sued the district, in part under Title IX of the Education Amendments of 1972, winning a jury award of almost half-a-million dollars. Pending the district's appeal to the Circuit Court, the case was settled for a similar amount, paid by the district's insurance company (see *Theno v. Tonganoxie Unified Sch. Dist. No. 464*, 377 F. Supp. 2d 952 (D. Kan. 2005).)

Find

A number of federal laws bar sexual harassment as a form of sex discrimination, including the U.S. Constitution's Fourteenth Amendment Equal Protection Clause, Title VII of the Civil Rights Act, and Title IX of the Education Laws of 1972. Also, different state and district formulations exist regarding sex discrimination, sexual orientation discrimination, harassment, bullying, and the like. This section focuses on rights under Title IX.

On January 19, 2001, OCR issued under Title IX "Revised Sexual Harassment Guidance: Harassment of Students by School Employees, Other Students, or Third Parties". The guidance defines sexual harassment under Title IX as "unwelcome conduct of a sexual nature. Sexual harassment can include unwelcome sexual advances, requests for sexual favors, and other verbal, nonverbal, or physical conduct of a sexual nature. Sexual harassment of a student can deny or limit, on the basis of sex, the student's ability to participate in or to receive benefits, services, or opportunities in the school's program."

The guidance followed landmark Title IX decisions by the Supreme Court in *Gebser v. Lago Vista Independent School District,* 524 U.S. 274 (1998) (district liability for employee–student harassment), and *Davis v. Monroe County Board of Education,* 526 U.S. 629 (1999) (district liability for student–student harassment). Under *Gebser,* district liability for damages under Title IX requires actual knowledge of the behavior by a district official who has authority to address the discrimination and can institute corrective measures on the victim's behalf. If, under these circumstances, the district exhibits "deliberate indifference" to the known offensive conduct, money damages may be judicially imposed.

The facts here require analysis under the student-to-student conditions of *Davis,* where the district was held liable for money damages under Title IX under the standards that (1) it was deliberately indifferent to the behavior, (2) it had actual knowledge under the *Gebser* definition, and (3) the harassment was so "severe, pervasive, and objectively offensive that it can be said to deprive the victims of access to the educational opportunities or benefits provided by the school."

In *Davis,* the fifth-grade female plaintiff had been subjected to a lengthy series of attempts by a male classmate to touch her breasts and genitals, and repeated vulgar statements. The Court explained the nature of actionable offenses by stating:

> Whether gender-oriented conduct rises to the level of actionable "harassment" thus "depends on a constellation of surrounding circumstances, expectations, and relationships," [citation omitted], including, but not limited to, the ages of the harasser and the victim and the number of individuals involved [citation omitted]. Courts, moreover, must bear in mind that schools are unlike the adult workplace and that children may regularly interact in a manner that would be unacceptable among adults. . . . Damages are not available for simple acts of teasing and name-calling among school children, however, even where these comments target differences in gender. Rather, in the context of student-on-student harassment, damages are available only where the behavior is so severe, pervasive, and objectively offensive that it denies its victims the equal access to education that Title IX is designed to protect.

OCR's standards for a finding of sexual harassment are somewhat different. In an OCR inquiry, at issue are not money damages but adherence to federal funding requirements. In one example where

OCR enforcement differs from judicial remedies for damages, OCR rejects the traditional judicial analysis that classifies sexual harassment within two strict categories: "quid pro quo" (conditioning a benefit on sexual conduct) or "hostile environment" (denying or limiting a student's ability to participate in or benefit from the school's program on the basis of sex). Instead, OCR maintains the terms but superimposes a series of inquiries on the fact pattern according to the type, frequency, and duration of the conduct and its objective and subjective impact on the victim.

Of particular importance, actual knowledge by a responsible administrator need not be proven under the OCR standard; rather, what is required is only proof that officials "knew or should have known" of the proscribed conduct. But, according to the guidance, "It is also important that schools not overreact to behavior that does not rise to the level of sexual harassment. As the Department stated in the 1997 guidance, a kiss on the cheek by a first grader does not constitute sexual harassment. School personnel should consider the age and maturity of students in responding to allegations of sexual harassment." Also, "It is important to recognize that Title IX's prohibition against sexual harassment does not extend to legitimate nonsexual touching or other nonsexual conduct."

As far back as 1990, OCR found that elementary school boys' sexual taunting of girls constituted sexual harassment (U.S. Department of Education, Office for Civil Rights [1993]. *Letter of Finding, Eden Prairie, Minn., Elementary School Sexual Harassment Incident,* Chicago, Ill.: U.S. Department of Education, Office of Civil Rights—Region V). Also, according to the current guidance,

> Although Title IX does not prohibit discrimination on the basis of sexual orientation, sexual harassment directed at gay or lesbian students that is sufficiently serious to limit or deny a student's ability to participate in or benefit from the school's program constitutes sexual harassment prohibited by Title IX under the circumstances described in this guidance. For example, if a male student or a group of male students target a gay student for physical

> sexual advances, serious enough to deny or limit the victim's ability to participate in or benefit from the school's program, the school would need to respond promptly and effectively, as described in this guidance, just as it would if the victim were heterosexual. On the other hand, if students heckle another student with comments based on the student's sexual orientation (e.g., "gay students are not welcome at this table in the cafeteria"), but their actions do not involve conduct of a sexual nature, their actions would not be sexual harassment covered by Title IX.

Thus, under the instant facts and despite the District Court's finding that the plaintiff stated a cause of action for student-to-student sexual harassment under Title IX, a violation of Title IX may not have occurred under the terms laid down by the nonenforceable but authoritative guidance. First, since the plaintiff was heterosexual according to the facts, no special consideration of sexual orientation is necessary. Second, unless the alleged threats were of a sexual nature, their mere utterance does not necessarily constitute "conduct of a sexual nature" under either judicial or administrative definitions of the term.

By settling, the insurance company representing the district may have avoided a more disadvantageous, sweeping decision by the Circuit Court but robbed us of an important precedent under Title IX.

Glossary

Academic freedom—the general ability of educators to teach and assign material free from political intimidation

Age Discrimination Act of 1975—prohibits discrimination on the basis of age in federally funded programs

Ambit—scope; breadth

Americans with Disabilities Act—prohibits discrimination on the basis of disability in employment, state and local government, public accommodations, commercial facilities, transportation, and telecommunications

Arbitrary and capricious the dual standard applied by courts to determine whether an administrative decision is illegal; opposite of the "rational basis" standard

Child Abuse Prevention and Treatment Act (CAPTA)—the main source of federal and state authority to regulate child abuse reporting by educators and other professionals

Civil Rights Act of 1964—the touchstone civil rights legislation of President Johnson's Great Society, which gave the federal government the right to enforce the constitutional right to vote; to protect against discrimination in public accommodations, public facilities, and public education; to prevent discrimination in federally assisted programs; to extend the Civil Rights Commission; and to establish the Equal Employment Opportunity Commission, among other initiatives, to guarantee racial equality within and among the states

De facto tenure—a system in which tenure is automatic and thus expected on the basis of teacher seniority

Due diligence—a series of investigatory steps consistent with professional requirements

Equal Protection Clause—the constitutional provision in Section 1 of the Fourteenth Amendment that guarantees equal protection on the basis of suspect classifications of race, religion, national origin, and belief, or with respect to fundamental rights such as freedom of speech, the press, and assembly

Executive committee—a committee of the board of directors or trustees, usually consisting of board officers, that provides leadership to the board and is given decision-making authority in the full board's absence

Gay baiting—taunts alleging homosexuality directed at straight or gay students, subject to Title IX enforcement

Grievance machinery—the procedures required when a teacher alleges a breach of contract by a school official, as when disciplinary charges are brought against the teacher

Legislative history—the committee reports, testimony, memoranda, floor speeches, and other material leading to legislative enactment, which that may be used to reveal its appropriate interpretation

Marketplace of ideas—the ideal of freely exchanged thoughts and opinions protected by the First Amendment

Office of Civil Rights (OCR)—the administrative agency, part of the U.S. Office of Education, empowered to enforce federal civil rights laws in federally funded education programs, including schools and higher education

Open meetings law—a statute requiring that public business be conducted in public session (*see* sunshine law)

Pretextual—describes a false but legally permissible reason put forth in place of the actual reason for an action, which may be illegal

Quasi-judicial bodies—an administrative body that acts in a judicial manner, rendering decisions on disagreements between two parties, but that is part of the executive branch rather than the judiciary

Rational basis—the standard courts use to determine whether an administrative determination should be upheld; opposite of impermissible "arbitrary and capricious" determinations

Reauthorize—to reenact a statute after it sunsets

Repeal—to withdraw a statute or regulation by official action

Section 504 of the Rehabilitation Act of 1973—prohibits discrimination on the basis of disability in federally funded programs

Sexual harassment—under Title IX, unwelcome conduct of a sexual nature

Sunset—the end a statute's authorized period of enforceability, requiring reauthorization if the statute is to continue in force (*see* reauthorize)

Sunshine law—a statute requiring that public business be conducted in public session or that government documents be available for public inspection (*see* open meetings law)

Tenure—the right to automatic contract renewal

Title IX of the Education Amendments of 1972—prohibits discrimination on the basis of gender in federally funded programs

CHAPTER FOUR

State and Federal Issues

Local educational agency (LEA)
generally, a school district

As described in chapter one, while states are the primary locus of power in American public education law, they delegate most decision-making authority to local school districts (called **local educational agencies [LEAs]** in most federal law). Thus, the focus of chapters two and three was on facts-and-find at the school and district levels, where most issues among students, parents, teachers, and school administrators are played out. The state's hand is present, but mostly hidden, as a guiding force in these controversies through its statutory and regulatory—call it policymaking—authority rather than through active decision-making on a case-by-case basis.

While not required under the Constitution, the federal government is increasingly partnering with states in educational policymaking, often with the states as reluctant participants. Using its constitutional funding powers under Article I, § 8, Congress inserts itself into the role traditionally left to the states to impose mandates on local districts. In accepting federal funds, arguably a Faustian bargain, the states become conduits for these federal programs. In passing along these obligations to LEAs, states often add their own regulatory requirements consistent with federal law. Even if the federal scheme is not fully funded (a situation called **unfunded mandates**) states, districts, and schools are required to fully comply with program requirements.

Unfunded mandate
the pejorative term for a federally required action by states and school districts without provision of sufficient federal funding to meet the requirements

Four of the most important federally imposed education laws are discussed in this chapter. Clearly, any of them could have been presented in the previous chapter since special education, No Child Left Behind (NCLB), and the Family Educational Rights and Privacy Act (FERPA) and Protection of Pupil Rights Amendment (PPRA) each touch students at the school and district levels. But they are best understood as policy pronouncements from Washington, filtered in somewhat differing forms through state education bureaucracies, before being implemented in thousands of districts around the country.

Since special education and NCLB are best understood as comprehensive policy programs rather than single, discrete legal obligations, the facts-and-find technique is temporarily abandoned here in favor of a more general approach that works better in thoroughly describing these subjects. No simple factual situation could possibly reveal the enormity of these multifaceted legal structures. If used here, facts-and-find would be as limiting as the proverbial blind man's description of an elephant. FERPA/PPRA, while still complex, is more conducive to the facts-and-find approach, so that technique will again be applied in the chapter's final section.

Special Education

Section 504 of the Rehabilitation Act
a federal statute barring discrimination against people with disabilities in federally funded programs

The federal law of special education is most clearly understood as a set of three separate statutes: **Section 504 of the Rehabilitation Act**; **P.L. 94–142** a.k.a. the **Education for All Handicapped Children Act (EAHCA)**, the **Education of the Handicapped Act (EHA)**, and the **Individuals with Disabilities Education Act** (IDEA), targeted at P-12 educational rights; and the **Americans with Disabilities Act (ADA).**

Americans with Disabilities Act (ADA)
statute requiring equal employment and physical accessibility for those with disabilities

Education for All Handicapped Children Act (EAHCA)
the original federal law establishing educational rights for students with disabilities

Education of the Handicapped Act (EHA) or P.L. 94–142
the Education of the Handicapped Act, which established the modern set of substantive and procedural rights enabling students with disabilities to receive free and appropriate public education

Individuals with Disabilities Education Act (IDEA)
the current version of the federal law mandating special education services for students with disabilities

Passed as part of the Rehabilitation Act of 1973, Section 504 prohibits discrimination against people with disabilities in programs supported by federal funds. Specifically, the law states: "No otherwise qualified individual with a handicap . . . shall solely by reason of her or his disability, be excluded from the participation in, be denied the benefits of, or be subjected to discrimination under any program or activity receiving federal financial assistance" (29 U.S.C. § 794).

As an antidiscrimination law, Section 504 exemplifies society's aspiration that people with handicaps should have equal rights. Title IX (see chapter three) is a similar law that guarantees equal treatment of women in all federally supported programs, though it should be noted that neither women nor people with handicaps are accorded the full protections of the Fourteenth Amendment's Equal Protection clause.

Section 504 is not specifically an education-related statute and actually grows out of a 1920 law that addressed employment and vocational rehabilitation. As a result, the definition of a person with a disability is not the same as the definition in IDEA, and includes "any person who (i) has a physical or mental impairment which substantially limits one or more of such person's major life activities [not just education], (ii) has a record of such an impairment, or (iii) is regarded as having such an impairment" (29 U.S.C. § 706(8)(B)). The major life activities referred to include "caring for one's self, performing manual tasks, walking, seeing, hearing, speaking, breathing, learning and working" (34 C.F.R. § 104.3(j)(2)(ii)). Thus, even students whose disability does not necessarily put them at an educational disadvantage, such as students using wheelchairs or those discharged from special education, can qualify under Section 504. Similarly, students who qualify under section 504 do not necessarily qualify for rights under IDEA.

The U.S. Department of Education's Office of Civil Rights (OCR) (see chapter three), rather than

Petitioner
the party initiating a civil action, particularly in an administrative proceeding

Limitations period
the time within which a legal action must be initiated

Respondent
the party required to respond to a civil action, particularly in an administrative proceeding

Related services
nonacademic interventions, such as occupational therapy and speech therapy, that permit students to gain from special education under the Individuals with Disabilities Education Act

Impartial hearing
a district-based proceeding initiated by a parent who disagrees with the school district's special education decision(s) concerning his or her child

individual plaintiffs, generally enforces Section 504. When an individual, called a **petitioner**, complains to OCR of an alleged misconduct within the 180-day **limitations period,** that agency investigates the matter and, if warranted, issues the appropriate order to correct the violation and/or assesses financial penalties against the violator. These rulings are, of course, subject to appeal by the alleged violator, usually called the **respondent** in these proceedings.

While the protected group of individuals covered by Section 504 is not as broad as those covered by ADA (Section 504 duties regulate only organizations receiving federal funds), the breadth of the protection against all discriminatory conduct provides sweeping rights for disabled students since most attend public schools in covered districts or receive federal funding for private education related to their disability. In many respects, Section 504 grants similar but less detailed rights to disabled students as those provided by IDEA. These include the right to a free appropriate public education, an accommodation plan, special educational and **related services,** and parent participation with an advocate in an **impartial hearing** to challenge district decisions regarding referral, evaluation, and placement.

The breadth of Section 504 and its roots in antidiscrimination have given rise to a separate body of precedent that sets it apart from IDEA litigation. For example, an important issue in these suits concerns which party bears the burden of proof. Under Section 504, the burden shifts to the respondent if the complainant can show that he or she is otherwise qualified for the benefit (an easy factual matter for disabled students) and that the benefit was denied. At that point, the school district or other party to the inquiry must show that the denial was for a reason other than the disability. This relatively low threshold makes Section 504 attractive to aggrieved parties, though its remedies may be less satisfying than those available through IDEA.

Section 504 is a precursor to the more detailed protections of IDEA and ADA but is more than a historical artifact. Case law arising from Section 504 litigation continues to provide general antidiscrimination protections for individuals with handicapping conditions outside the public education and employment contexts. For example, students with handicapping conditions in a religious school that accepts federal Title I funds are protected by Section 504, even without going through the referral, evaluation, and placement procedures mandated by IDEA.

IDEA defines a student as within its protected class if she or he needs special education or related services such as speech or occupational therapy because of mental retardation, hearing impairments (including deafness), speech or language impairments, visual impairments (including blindness), serious emotional disturbance, orthopedic impairments, autism, traumatic brain injury, other health impairments, or specific learning disabilities.

IDEA and its supporting regulations maintain the primary rights to a free, appropriate education established by its predecessor, EAHCA, while making major changes to important secondary rights concerning attorneys' fees, discipline, private education, and funding. The two statutes are often incorrectly used interchangeably to generically identify all federally guaranteed rights of handicapped students.

IDEA is the current version of an older statute, P.L. 94–142, which was passed in 1975 and became effective in 1977. All bills passed by Congress have a "P.L." number that identifies the Congress that passed them (in this case the 94th Session of Congress) and their position in the sequence of bills passed in that session (in this case, the 142nd bill of the 94th Congress). This system is used because different parts of bills are often separated when published in the United States Code. To locate how those parts fit together in the original legislation, the P.L number is used.

To make special education nomenclature even more confusing, P.L. 94–142 is also called the Education for All Handicapped Children Act (EAHCA). That law was an amendment to the Education of the

Handicapped Act (EHA) passed in 1970. Technically, the EHA, EAHCA, and PL 94–142 refer only to those particular bills. The original P.L. 94–142 and regulations immediately derived from it have been amended often since initial passage. Thus, their texts should not be regarded as current law—as of this writing, the current law is IDEA. IDEA, incorporating its subsequent amendments in 1997 and 2004, has become the touchstone for analyzing the rights of all publicly funded special education students in the United States.

The actual text of P.L. 94–142 is of interest mainly as a historical marker to note early federal efforts that specifically guaranteed disabled students educational rights and provided the original legislative endorsement for many rights that exist today.

This helps us understand that the underpinnings of special education lie in the civil rights movement. P.L. 94–142 was basically a civil rights statute and is best understood in the context of the post–*Brown v. Board of Education* drive to secure equal rights for what that decision described as "discrete and insular" groups, which, because they are inherently in the minority, are often disadvantaged by majority rule. With the Civil Rights Act of 1964, the movement for African American civil rights showed that it could successfully transfer its efforts from the federal courts to Congress. Similarly, after victories by the special education advocacy community during the early 1970s in such cases as *PARC I* and *II* (see below), these organizations seized their momentum by successfully securing federal educational rights for the disabled through P.L. 94–142 where they had been previously stymied by state courts and legislatures.

Before the EAHCA, students with disabilities were regularly excluded from public education unless specifically provided for by state law. This situation began to change with *Pennsylvania Association for Retarded Children v. Commonwealth of Pennsylvania,* 334 F.Supp. 1257 (E.D. Pa. 1971) (*PARC I*) and 343 F. Supp. 279 (E.D. Pa. 1972) (*PARC II*), and when parents alleged that Pennsylvania had a state constitutional duty to educate all children. In an influential consent decree (a settlement agreement between the parties that becomes a court order), Pennsylvania agreed that students with disabilities had due process and equal protection rights to a free public education and that placement in a regular classroom (i.e., the **least restrictive environment [LRE]**) was preferable to self-contained instructional programs.

P.L. 94–142 was notable for requiring that all states accepting federal special education funds provide handicapped students in public schools with a **free and appropriate public education (FAPE)** according to an **individualized educational program (IEP)** in the least restrictive environment, under strict regulations of the U.S. Department of Education that include a **30/60-day time line** requiring school districts to provide students referred for special education with evaluations within 30 days and placement within 60 days of referral. These provisions are now part of IDEA.

Every student identified as handicapped under IDEA is required to have an IEP that establishes the educational and related services required by the student to make appropriate educational progress. The IEP is essentially a contract between the district and the parents of the handicapped student that establishes legal rights though no monetary remedy if breached. Failure of districts to meet these requirements can result in students being placed by parents in private schools without prior district approval, with the district footing the bill.

The statute also establishes **mainstreaming** as the favored placement. This requires placement of a handicapped student in general education for all or part of the school day, since this is considered the least restrictive environment of all. Partially because it is often cheaper to place students in regular classrooms, even with individual aides, and because the law requires it, districts may attempt to place children in the mainstream, while, ironically, parents sometimes seek more segregated placements, believ-

Least restrictive environment (LRE)
the precept that students in special education should be placed in the most mainstream instructional setting possible appropriate to their ability to learn

Free and appropriate public education (FAPE)
the basic right of students with disabilities established by the Education for All Handicapped Children Act, Education of the Handicapped Act, and Individuals with Disabilities Education Act

Individualized educational program (IEP)
the required instructional plan for a child in special education to achieve learning objectives

30/60-day time line
the Individuals with Disabilities Education Act requirement that districts evaluate a student's educational needs within 30 days of referral and place the student in an appropriate setting within 60 days of referral

Mainstreaming
placing students with disabilities with general education students

ing their children will get more individual, professional, IEP-targeted attention than in regular classrooms. As a result, mainstreaming remains an elusive goal. The merits of mainstreaming are thus most constructively debated on a case-by-case basis rather than, as frequently occurs, on an ideological policy level.

"Stay put" provision the Individuals with Disabilities Education Act requirement that students in special education have a right to keep their current placement pending a final decision to change placement

IDEA also requires that a handicapped student continue in his or her current educational placement while any review proceedings are taking place before a change in placement. This **"stay put" provision** has prevented many unilateral changes in students' placement by school districts over parent and student objections, especially pending review of students' placement in expensive private settings at district expense.

Similarly, the stay put provision is generally in force in the area of student discipline. Whether school districts retain disciplinary authority over students in special education was addressed in *Honig, California Superintendent of Public Instruction v. Doe,* 484 U.S. 305 (1988). The Supreme Court ruled that in cases where the inappropriate conduct is a result of the handicapping condition (such as emotional disturbance), districts could not unilaterally exclude the student for an indeterminate amount of time. This ruling is sometimes misinterpreted to preclude any discipline of students in special education, but this is incorrect. *Honig* and subsequent amendment of IDEA permit short-term suspensions up to ten days and other similar measures to protect the safety of the student and others. Any suspension for more than ten days would be regarded as a change of placement, requiring reconvening of the Committee on Special Education.

A continuing frustration of general education practitioners has been this clear direction that students with disabilities not be punished for improper conduct arising from their condition, even if the student has not been formally identified as requiring special education or related services. Before a district can impose substantial disciplinary action against a stu-

Manifestation determination review
a proceeding to ascertain whether the cause for disciplinary action arises from a student's handicapping condition, in which case such discipline is not permissible

dent eligible for special education, it is required to conduct a **manifestation determination review.** The objective is to assess whether the improper conduct was precipitated by the student's disability and whether the IEP, within the context of a continuing preference for the least restrictive environment, requires modification in light of the inappropriate conduct. An important change in the 2004 IDEA amendment now requires that the parent prove that the inappropriate conduct arose from the handicapping condition. Previously, the burden was on the district to prove that the behavior was not a manifestation of the condition. Hearings have also become easier for districts to win with the elimination of a provision requiring consideration of whether the disability impaired the child's ability to control or to understand the impact and consequences of the behavior. Parents may appeal the outcome of the manifestation determination review if they disagree with the outcome through further due process hearings.

In attempting to reconcile the inevitable disputes between parents and districts over the referral, evaluation, and placement of students, IDEA provides for the nonjudicial remedy of an impartial hearing. At its most basic level, such a dispute occurs when parents do not believe their child has a disability but the teacher disagrees. The impartial hearing, though not as procedurally complex as an appeal to the federal courts that may follow, has been an enduring source of vexation to both parties, because of the highly personal issues involved and their monetary stakes, including entitlement to attorney's fees if the parent prevails.

As part of its character as civil rights legislation, IDEA requires public funding for special needs students on a par with other public school students. But many view special education funding as the quintessential "unfunded mandate" that state and local governments, including school districts, complain about when Congress creates requirements that other government entities must meet.

Compliance with federal special education requirements is extremely expensive for school districts. While under constitutional precepts it is understood that states and districts have a general duty to provide for the education of all public school students, the particular requirements of the federal legislation have placed enormous financial burdens on local and state budgets. Since these obligations are not fully covered by federal funds, special education has been continually criticized as unfairly shifting the financial consequences of implementation to governmental bodies having no say in the laws' creation.

When EAHCA was enacted, Congress intended that the federal government would carry 40 percent of the cost of students' special education services. However, the federal share has never topped 20 percent of need, and for most of the past quarter century only between 7 and 12 percent has been allocated. Thus, the ever-burgeoning special education budget has become largely a state and local burden.

The reason for the nonfederal responsibility is best understood in terms of the well-known IDEA requirement that students with disabilities receive a free appropriate public education just as children in general education receive publicly funded education from local districts and state aid. In return for federal financial assistance, state education agencies enter into an agreement to meet the FAPE requirement that mandates payment for educational services and related services that make it possible for the student to profit from a special education. Even funds that a parent may require to vindicate a student's right to special educational services are covered.

In *Board of Education of Hendrick Hudson Central School District v. Rowley,* 458 U.S. 176 (1982), the Supreme Court established the ceiling for a school district's FAPE obligations. The parents of Amy Rowley, a kindergarten student with a severe hearing impairment, sued the Hendrick. Hudson Central School District when they provided her with an FM hearing aid. Her parents asserted that she required a sign language interpreter to maximize her educational potential in a manner similar to nondisabled students. The Supreme Court disagreed, holding that EAHCA was not intended "to achieve strict equity services for handicapped and nonhandicapped children." Instead, the school district was permitted to provide the lesser service since that would enable Amy "to benefit" from her placement, thus satisfying the law's requirement of an "appropriate education."

Obligations related to a free, appropriate education are not limited to a student's instructional needs. Under IDEA, school districts are required to provide qualified students with "related services." According to Congress, related services include "medical and counseling services, except that such medical services shall be for diagnostic and placement purposes only as may be required to assist a handicapped child to benefit from special education." *Irving Independent School District v. Tatro,* 468 U.S. 883 (1984), addressed the question of whether the district was required to provide regular catheterization to a student with spina bifida who could not voluntarily empty her bladder. The Supreme Court held that since (1) the student qualified for related services, (2) the related service was necessary for her to benefit from her appropriate educational placement, (3) the procedure could be carried out by a school nurse rather than a doctor, and (4) it could be done without specialized equipment, the district was required to fund the necessary care.

Why do states enter into this fiscally disadvantageous agreement? Basically, because political and ethical forces oblige them to provide for children with special needs and the federal dollars, while fewer than states might like, provide needed assistance, amounting to almost $10.6 billion in FY2006. Two issues face the federal government, states, and districts regarding the funding of special education under IDEA. The first is the gross amount of federal dollars allocated under the law. Consistent with the national model of education funding of the general population, the education of disabled students is largely a state and local responsibility. At the same time, Congress has long acknowledged the goal to fund 40 percent of the national average per pupil expenditure for students in special education because of the increased burdens of IDEA compliance. This goal has yet to be met, although the 2004 amendment seeks to achieve "full" funding of the 40 percent federal share by 2010. Second, the 1997 IDEA amendments sought to achieve greater equity in the allocation formula among states and districts for special education costs. This may be achieved by replacing the previous child count emphasis with census data and accounting more accurately for district needs and ability to pay. Districts were also provided with greater flexibility to share costs of assistive technology, related services, and similar expenses.

As with other public education responsibilities, states and localities are not permitted to pass along special education costs to families. Even for well-off families who might normally send their children to private school, if no timely appropriate placement is made by the district in public school, the Supreme Court has ruled that the district is responsible for funding the child's private education.

In *Florence County School District Four v. Carter,* 510 U.S. 7 (1993), the continuing battle by school districts to minimize their financial obligations under IDEA suffered a severe setback. The Supreme Court held that where a district fails to provide adequate public placement, parents are entitled to full reimbursement of tuition when they place their child in an appropriate private setting without prior district approval (often called a "unilateral," or one-sided, placement). One consequence of the *Carter* decision has been a growing movement by wealthier families to find expensive private placements, initially pay tuition out-of-pocket, then sue the district for ***Carter* funding,** using expensive evaluators and lawyers to make the case for inappropriate public placement. Obviously, poorer families cannot wait months and years paying private school tuition and hoping for later reimbursement.

***Carter* funding**
public financing of students in special education who have been placed in private schools by parents pending district determination of placement options

Florence County School District Four v. Carter, 510 U.S. 7 (1993) [some text omitted]

Justice O'Connor delivered the opinion of the Court.

Respondent Shannon Carter was classified as learning disabled in 1985, while a ninth grade student in a school operated by petitioner Florence County School District Four. School officials met with Shannon's parents to formulate an individualized education program (IEP) for Shannon, as required under IDEA. The IEP provided that Shannon would stay in regular classes except for three periods of individualized instruction per week, and established specific goals in reading and mathematics of four months' progress for the entire school year. Shannon's parents were dissatisfied, and requested a hearing to challenge the appropriateness of the IEP. Both the local educational officer and the state educational agency hearing officer rejected Shannon's parents' claim and concluded that the IEP was adequate. In the meantime, Shannon's parents had placed her in Trident Academy, a private school specializing in educating children with disabilities. Shannon began at Trident in September 1985 and graduated in the spring of 1988.

Shannon's parents filed this suit in July 1986, claiming that the school district had breached its duty under IDEA to provide Shannon with a "free appropriate public education," § 1401(a)(18), and seeking reimbursement for tuition and other costs incurred at Trident. After a bench trial, the District Court ruled in the parents' favor. The court held that the school district's proposed educational program and the achievement goals of the IEP "were wholly inadequate" and failed to satisfy the requirements of the Act. The court further held that "[a]lthough [Trident Academy] did not comply with all of the procedures outlined in [IDEA]," the school "provided Shannon an excellent education in substantial compliance with all the substantive requirements" of the statute. The court found that Trident "evaluated Shannon quarterly, not yearly as mandated in [IDEA], it provided Shannon with low teacher student ratios, and it developed a plan which allowed Shannon to receive passing marks and progress from grade to grade." The court also credited the findings of its own expert, who determined that Shannon had made "significant progress" at Trident and that her reading comprehension had risen three grade levels in her three years at the school. The District Court concluded that Shannon's education was "appropriate" under IDEA, and that Shannon's parents were entitled to reimbursement of tuition and other costs.

The Court of Appeals for the Fourth Circuit affirmed. The court agreed that the IEP proposed by the school district was inappropriate under IDEA. It also rejected the school district's argument that reimbursement is never proper when the parents choose a private school that is not approved by the State or that does not comply with all the terms of IDEA. According to the Court of Appeals, neither the text of the Act nor its legislative history imposes a "requirement that the private school be approved by the state in parent placement reimbursement cases." To the contrary, the Court of Appeals concluded, IDEA's state approval requirement applies only when a child is placed in a private school by public school officials. Accordingly, "when a public school system has defaulted on its obligations under the Act, a private school placement is 'proper under the Act' if the education provided by the private school is 'reasonably calculated to enable the child to receive educational benefits.'" quoting *Board of Ed. of Hendrick Hudson Central School Dist.* v. *Rowley,* 458 U.S. 176, 207 (1982).

The court below recognized that its holding conflicted with *Tucker* v. *Bay Shore Union Free School Dist.,* 873 F. 2d 563, 568 (1989), in which the Court of Appeals for the Second Circuit held that parental placement in a private school cannot be proper under the Act unless the private school in question meets the standards of the state education agency. In *School Comm. of Burlington* v. *Department of Ed. of Mass.,* 471 U.S. 359, 369 (1985), we held that IDEA's grant of equitable authority empowers a court "to order school authorities to reimburse parents for their expenditures on private special education for a child if the court ultimately determines that such placement, rather than a proposed IEP, is proper under the Act." Congress intended that IDEA's promise of a "free appropriate public education" for disabled children would normally be met by an IEP's provision for education in the regular public schools or in private schools chosen jointly by school officials and parents. In cases where cooperation fails, however, "parents who disagree with the proposed IEP are faced with a choice: go along with the IEP to the detriment of their child if it turns out to be inappropriate or pay for what they consider to be the appropriate placement." For parents willing and able to make the latter choice, "it would be an empty victory to have a court tell them several years later that they were right but that these expenditures could not in a proper case be reimbursed by the school officials." *Ibid.* Because such a result would be contrary to IDEA's guarantee of a "free appropriate public education," we held that "Congress meant to include retroactive reimbursement to parents as an available remedy in a proper case."

As this case comes to us, two issues are settled: 1) the school district's proposed IEP was inappropriate under IDEA, and 2) although Trident did not meet the §1401(a)(18) requirements, it provided an education otherwise proper under IDEA. This case presents the narrow question whether Shannon's parents are barred from reimbursement because the private school in which Shannon enrolled did not meet the § 1401(a)(18) definition of a "free appropriate public education." We hold that they are not, because §1401(a)(18)'s requirements cannot be read as applying to parental placements.

Section 1401(a)(18)(A) requires that the education be "provided at public expense, under public supervision and direction." Similarly, § 1401(a)(18)(D) requires schools to provide an IEP, which must be designed by "a representative of the local educational agency," 20 U.S.C. § 1401(a)(20) (1988 ed., Supp. IV), and must be "establish[ed]," "revise[d]," and "review[ed]" by the agency, § 1414(a)(5). These requirements do not make sense in the context of a parental placement. In this case, as in all *Burlington* reimbursement cases, the parents' rejection of the school district's proposed IEP is the very reason for the parents' decision to put their child in a private school. In such cases, where the private placement has necessarily been made over the school district's objection, the private school education will not be under "public supervision and direction." Accordingly, to read the §1401(a)(18) requirements as applying to parental placements would effectively eliminate the right of unilateral withdrawal recognized in *Burlington*. Moreover, IDEA was intended to ensure that children with disabilities receive an education that is both appropriate and free. *Burlington, supra,* at 373. To read the provisions of §1401(a)(18) to bar reimbursement in the circumstances of this case would defeat this statutory purpose.

Nor do we believe that reimbursement is necessarily barred by a private school's failure to meet state education standards. Trident's deficiencies, according to the school district, were that it employed at least two faculty members who were not state certified and that it did not develop IEPs. Accordingly, we disagree with the Second Circuit's theory that "a parent may not obtain reimbursement for a unilateral placement if that placement was in a school that was not on [the State's] approved list of private" schools. Parents' failure to select a program known to be approved by the State in favor of an unapproved option is not itself a bar to reimbursement.

Furthermore, although the absence of an approved list of private schools is not essential to our holding, we note that parents in the position of Shannon's have no way of knowing at the time they select a private school whether the school meets state standards. South Carolina keeps no publicly available list of approved private schools, but instead approves private school placements on a case by case basis. In fact, although public school officials had previously placed three children with disabilities at Trident, Trident had not received blanket approval from the State. South Carolina's case by case approval system meant that Shannon's parents needed the cooperation of state officials before they could know whether Trident was state approved. As we recognized in *Burlington,* such cooperation is unlikely in cases where the school officials disagree with the need for the private placement. 471 U. S., at 372.

The school district also claims that allowing reimbursement for parents such as Shannon's puts an unreasonable burden on financially strapped local educational authorities. The school district argues that requiring parents to choose a state approved private school if they want reimbursement is the only meaningful way to allow States to control costs; otherwise States will have to reimburse dissatisfied parents for any private school that provides an education that is proper under the Act, no matter how expensive it may be.

There is no doubt that Congress has imposed a significant financial burden on States and school districts that participate in IDEA. Yet public educational authorities who want to avoid reimbursing parents for the private education of a disabled child can do one of two things: give the child a free appropriate public education in a public setting, or place the child in an appropriate private setting of the State's choice. This is IDEA's mandate, and school officials who conform to it need not worry about reimbursement claims.

Moreover, parents who, like Shannon's, "unilaterally change their child's placement during the pendency of review proceedings, without the consent of the state or local school officials, do so at their own financial risk." *Burlington, supra,* at 373–374. They are entitled to reimbursement *only* if a federal court concludes both that the public placement violated IDEA, and that the private school placement was proper under the Act.

Accordingly, we affirm the judgment of the Court of Appeals.

Significant issues involved in unilateral, preferential placement of students with disabilities in private and charter schools were resolved by the 1997 IDEA amendments. Students receiving private place-

ments as a result of a district's IEP determination of a free, appropriate public education or in lieu of an appropriate district placement are entitled to full public funding. Similarly, students in charter schools, since they are public, receive free educational services according to their IEP. But, according to 20 U.S.C. § 1412 (a)(10)(A)(i)(I), where a placement is wholly based on a parent's desire for private schooling and an appropriate public setting exists, the student is eligible for publicly funded services proportionate to what the federal share of the district's expenses would be if the child attended public school.

Another question that arose with respect to special education funding was the right of students with special needs attending religious schools to receive publicly financed assistance. This intersection of special education and the First Amendment's separation of church and state was addressed in *Zobrest v. Catalina Foothills School District,* 509 U.S. 1 (1993). The question presented to the Supreme Court was whether a hearing-impaired high school student attending parochial school was entitled to public funding for a sign language interpreter, consistent with his IEP. The Court ruled that IDEA required that the school district provide the interpreter, since it was part of a neutral government service that did not advance the religious message of the school. In addition, the placement of the public employee on religious school grounds did not present a sufficient appearance of government support of religion to violate the Establishment Clause.

Attorneys' fees under IDEA were taken up by Congress through the 1986 Handicapped Children's Protection Act (HCPA) after the Supreme Court in *Smith v. Robinson,* 468 U.S. 992 (1984), ruled that fees could not be recovered under EAHCA. The issue was revisited in the 1997 IDEA reauthorization. As a general matter, courts are permitted to award attorneys' fees to parents of children with disabilities when the parents are the prevailing party to the action, although the issue of whether parents have "prevailed" is often a matter of separate dispute between the parent's attorney and the school district, as are the particular legal work and rates involved. School districts can also be awarded attorneys' fees by the parent if the action is determined to be frivolous. The statute attempts to balance the right of parents to reasonable fees with an interest in early settlement.

The last in the main trio of federal statutes related to students with special needs is ADA. Passed in 1990, the Americans with Disabilities Act, PL 101–336, 42 U.S.C. § 12101 *et seq.*, was not specifically intended to address the requirements of students for special education but rather seeks to eliminate discrimination against handicapped individuals generally, including some arguably outside of other statutes' protections, such as people with contagious diseases and those who are associated with someone with a handicapping condition (e.g., a student with an infirm parent). Clearly, the AIDS epidemic was on legislators' minds when crafting this expansive definition of handicap.

In this way, ADA more closely resembles the broad protections of Section 504 of the Rehabilitation Act than IDEA. This is particularly important for students in private K-12 education (except insofar as there may be a public school placement) and in higher education, where the requirements of IDEA usually don't reach. Also, while the remedies available under IDEA do not correct past violations, ADA claims can include demands for reasonable accommodation in the future as well as more traditional monetary damages for past harm.

Finally, ADA's focus on public accommodation and employment discrimination brought important new constituencies into the fight for equal rights for all handicapped individuals. Prior to ADA, for example, appeals for architectural barrier removal in schools, public transportation, and the like were often fought on the relatively more narrow grounds of Section 504 and IDEA compliance. With the advent of ADA, however, these issues became the province of workers, the elderly, and those with covered medical conditions. Through their efforts, and the work of their attorneys, new energy and horizons were added to the special education advocacy community.

Passage of ADA also completed the current "trinity" of federal statutory law protecting the interests of students in special education: Section 504, IDEA (PL 94–142 as amended), and ADA. Each statute, while containing overlapping rights for disabled students, has its unique protections and case precedents. Parties must dig through each legal quarry to ascertain the best strategies for successful resolution of special education disputes.

No Child Left Behind and Title I

The No Child Left Behind Act of 2001 (NCLB), P.L. 107–110, contains the most recent amendments to the Elementary and Secondary Education Act of 1965 (ESEA), including **Title I,** the most extensive and expensive federal education program, which is targeted to assist low-income students. Since Congress passed ESEA as part of President Johnson's War on Poverty, the role of the federal government in education has expanded. The 2001 reauthorization of ESEA, renamed NCLB, was clearly the most dramatic change in national school legislation since ESEA's inception. NCLB moved the federal government from being primarily a source of funding (now about 9 percent of every public school dollar) to being a major actor in shaping the substance of K-12 instruction. By providing federal assistance for remediation in high-poverty schools, Title I has been used to impose annual testing and other accountability measures on all U.S. public schools.

Title I
the major federal education legislation targeted to assist low-income students but now subsumed within the broader mandates of No Child Left Behind

For the first time, the federal government has required a framework for creating state standards, testing, and accountability—an apparatus new to federal education legislation. This structure extends from the child to subgroups of children, to the school, the district, and the state. This level of standardization removes discretion from the local community, vesting control in a system that is quite new to American education.

NCLB's stated objective is to ensure that all public school students in the United States meet high academic standards by 2014, including traditionally underserved groups such as low-income students, black and Latino students, students with limited English proficiency (LEP), and those requiring special education services.

Adequate yearly progress (AYP)
the main standard of school and district progress under the No Child Left Behind Act

Safe harbor
under the accountability provisions of No Child Left Behind, states, school districts, and schools may still make adequate yearly progress if each subgroup that fails to reach its proficiency performance targets is reduced by 10 percent of the previous year's percentage if other targets are met

Supplementary educational services (SES)
the right of students under No Child Left Behind to receive free tutoring and other after-school instruction if their schools fails to make adequate yearly progress two years in row

Scientifically based research (SBR)
the requirement under No Child Left Behind that instructional materials be validated as promoting student learning

Progress toward this goal is measured by **adequate yearly progress (AYP)** in meeting state standards through annual tests in reading, math, and science for all students in grades K-8, along with high school indicators. Test data are disaggregated by grade and the specific populations described above. Except for so-called **safe harbor** exemptions, districts and schools receiving federal Title I funding that fail to make AYP two or more years in a row in the disaggregated categories created by the law (e.g., third grade reading scores of Latino students) are sanctioned by imposition of parent-initiated school choice, **supplementary educational services (SES)** such as tutoring, and curricula validated by **scientifically based research (SBR),** as approved by the federal Department of Education. NCLB also requires that 95 percent of every sizable cohort be tested, and if an insufficient number fail to sit for the exam, NCLB assumes failure to make AYP for the entire cohort based on a three-year average. Extended failure to make AYP results in schools' reorganization or, ultimately, closure or takeover by the state or a private management company. While NCLB imposes rigorous demands on states and localities, case law so far does not provide parents or students with a private right of action to enforce its provisions (*Association of Community Organizations for Reform Now (ACORN) v. New York City Department of Education,* 269 F.Supp.2d 338 (S.D.N.Y. 2003)).

According to the U.S. Department of Education, the sanctions or "School Improvement Options" given in Table 1 follow upon two years of failure to meet AYP requirements. "Year 1" thus begins in the

TABLE 1: SCHOOL IMPROVEMENT OPTIONS

	A school is identified for school improvement after it has not made AYP for two consecutive school years. A school moves to the next "step" or "year" in this chart if it continues to not make AYP.
School Improvement (Year One)	In general, schools identified for improvement must receive technical assistance that enables them to specifically address the academic achievement problem that caused the school to be identified for improvement. The LEA is required to provide technical assistance as the school develops and implements the plan, including specific assistance in analyzing assessment data, improving professional development, and improving resource allocation. In addition, the following must take place: 1. All students are offered public school choice. 2. Each school identified for improvement must develop or revise a two-year school improvement plan, in consultation with parents, school staff, the local educational agency, and other experts, for approval by the LEA. The plan must incorporate research-based strategies, a 10 percent set-aside of Title I funds for professional development, extended learning time as appropriate (including school day or year), strategies to promote effective parental involvement and mentoring for new teachers.
School Improvement, (Year Two)	1. Make available supplemental educational services to students from low-income families. *In addition, the LEA continues to offer technical assistance to implement the new plan, and offer public school choice.*
Corrective Action (Year Three)	Corrective Action requires an LEA to take actions likely to bring about meaningful change at the school. To accomplish this goal, LEAs are required to take at least one of the following corrective actions, depending on the needs of the individual school: 1. Replace school staff responsible for the continued failure to make AYP; 2. Implement a new curriculum based on scientifically based research (including professional development); 3. Significantly decrease management authority at the school level; 4. Extend the school day or school year; 5. Appoint an outside expert to advise the school on its progress toward making AYP in accordance with its school plan; OR 6. Reorganize the school internally. *In addition, the LEA continues to offer technical assistance public school choice, and supplemental educational services.*
Restructuring (Year Four)	During the first year of restructuring, the LEA is required to prepare a plan and make necessary arrangements to carry out one of the following options: 1. Reopen school as charter school. 2. Replace principal and staff. 3. Contract for private management company of demonstrated effectiveness. 4. State takeover. 5. Any other major restructuring of school governance. *In addition, the LEA continues to offer public school choice and supplemental educational services.*
Implementation of Restructuring (Year Five)	Implement alternative governance plan no later than first day of school year following year four described above.

Source: U.S. Dept. of of Education

school year following the second straight year of failure to meet AYP.

Thus the statute insinuates itself into the day-to-day operation of schools, requiring that students make AYP or subjecting their schools and districts to progressively more onerous sanctions. For the first time in our history, the federal government is demanding that states set standards, test students, report results by student, type, school and district, and establish consequences for schools and students who fail to show adequate yearly progress.

NCLB moves the United States toward a national standard in education, based on state-determined standards and tests, along with a set of processes and consequences that are federally mandated. The process is complex and expensive; it involves the setting of state standards, the alignment of standards with curricula and yearly testing, the determination of inadequate and proficient levels of subject mastery, the application of the same standards to all students without regard to their initial academic proficiency to show AYP based on 2001–2002 benchmarks, and consequences, including the loss of administrative federal funding, for states that cannot or will not comply.

The "secret weapon" of standardization is the National Assessment of Educational Progress (NAEP), against which state test results are compared to see whether states are dumbing-down their tests to look better on national comparisons. If state proficiency levels are upwardly skewed and fail to match student progress on the now-compulsory NAEP, state standards will be found wanting by the Department of Education and sanctions will be imposed, including statewide withholding of Title I funds.

Even with comparison of state standards to NAEP, the very idea of state autonomy in setting standards presages continuing disparities in test difficulty. For examples, eavesdrop on some of my recent email:

> I'll trade them [State A's] system for [State B's] and I'll throw in tips for making the number game go the way you want it to;

> I am an elementary teacher who moved to [State C] from [State D] last year, having been totally persuaded by the state's hype about radical improvement. I'll cut to the chase and tell you the [State C] tests are absurdly easy compared to those in [State D];

> I encourage everyone to put [State E's] Test in your search engine and look at what [State E] uses for their state proficiency where everyone is doing so well. Compare a [State E] 8–10th grade test to an [State F] 4th grade proficiency test. Your jaw will fall open when you see how much more difficult [State F's] elementary level test is in comparison to the [State E] high school test. This is why [State F] is ranking low by Federal standards. Our standards are too high. (Students must score about 81% to pass.)

The problem is that making AYP across every cohort, every year, is almost impossible. Educators and learners reflecting on the reality of student progress know that achievement is always fitful, at best a two steps forward–one step back struggle that is at once exhilarating and frustrating. On testing days, an individual student may not be two steps ahead. And if most of that student's cohort (assuming 95 percent show up) are in a similar position, their school will be at risk of failing AYP. Even if the group measures up the next year, another cohort's off-day may give the school two years of failure, and on and on, toward reorganization.

Use of scientifically based research in curriculum selection for Title I schools is another NCLB provision of importance to students, parents, and special educators. The standards used to ascertain the qualities that meet the federal requirement have yet to be clearly determined, but a small industry is likely to arise to assess and promote materials that purport to meet the NCLB standard.

Under the term "scientifically based research," which appears more than one hundred times in the Act, districts are required to promote student learning to the exclusion of non-SBR techniques. But already journal ads are full of self-professed SBR claims with questionable validity. In the absence of an agreed-upon standard for instructional materials (such as the Federal Drug Administration provides for medicine or the Underwriters Laboratory provides for product compliance), the SBR requirement is little more than a label. The truth is that conclusive SBR findings are rare. Science, after all, is a process of constant hypothesis testing, not static truths. What works often depends on very specific conditions and narrow experimental groups. Classrooms of students are not patients whose medication can be determined and prescribed individually. And even the safest, most effective prescriptions don't work with everyone. But the annual testing regime of NCLB leaves no time for such trial and error.

Special education is a particularly thorny part of NCLB, with extra challenges for educators and families alike. Along with other students in grades 3–8, NCLB requires states to annually test students with disabilities in math, reading, and eventually science. According to Department of Education guidance issued in December 2005, regarding "Students with Disabilities and Modified Achievement Standards," the same tests are given to all students, except that a maximum of 2 percent of students with special needs (those receiving services under IDEA) who achieve proficiency using alternative assessments may be counted by districts as making AYP. These alternative assessments differ from the grade-level tests taken by most students and are specially aligned to determine academic performance apart from students' handicapping condition. For students with the most significant cognitive impairments, the alternative assessments measure individual instructional level apart from grade-level norms.

Scores for special education students in each school must still show adequate yearly progress from year to year. If special education students do not make AYP according to state standards, the school may be subject to sanctions as when other scores fall short. One of many complexities in the law, however, is that while schools often fail to meet standards because they do not address the educational needs of disabled students, the underserved special education students are often prevented from taking advantage of NCLB's school choice provision because other district schools do not have classes to meet their needs.

Another problem is the inherent conflict between the goals of IDEA and of NCLB. NCLB holds all students, schools, and districts to a common statewide definition of academic achievement and favors adoption of district-wide curricula based on SBR. IDEA, on the other hand, favors an individualized approach to achievement and methodologies through the IEP. Further, the two statutes' different testing and reporting requirements and timetables (annually for NCLB, biannually for IDEA) are confusing and may cause parents and districts to standardize special education instruction to meet the demands of NCLB, to the detriment of IDEA compliance.

Computation of AYP for specialized populations might have two different perverse effects on referrals to special education. Since AYP is calculated on the basis of percentages of students from different groups meeting standards, administrators may be tempted to keep students eligible for special education in general education, where their scores, if lower than the general population's, will be "hidden" within the larger denominator. On the other hand, administrators might over-refer in order to create an artificially high-performing special education cohort, thus avoiding that disaggregated group from falling below levels of AYP and triggering school or district sanctions.

Highly qualified teacher the No Child Left Behind requirement that all students will be taught by certified teachers

Another provision of the law, requiring what the statute calls a **highly qualified teacher** in every classroom, was one of the first mandates to be amended so that special education teachers do not have to be subject-area specialists, as originally required. According to the Department of Education's March 2004 guidance on the subject, NCLB's highly qualified teacher requirements "apply only to teachers providing direct instruction in core academic subjects. Special educators who do not directly instruct students in core academic subjects or who provide only consultation to highly qualified teachers in adapting curricula, using behavioral supports and interventions or selecting appropriate accommodations, do not need to demonstrate subject-matter competency in those subjects."

Family Educational Rights and Privacy Act (FERPA)
the "Buckley Amendment," which provides privacy protections for identifiable student records

This brief guide to Title I provisions of NCLB only scratches the surface of this complex statute, which, no doubt, will be extensively amended when it is extended, then reauthorized, after its 2007 sunset year. For greater detail, please refer to *No Child Left Behind Primer* by Frederick M. Hess and Michael J. Petrilli (Peter Lang, 2007).

The Family Educational Rights and Privacy Act and the Protection of Pupil Rights Amendment

Protection of Pupil Rights Amendment (PPRA)
often called the "Hatch Amendment," the law provides for student and parent access to review instructional materials and to opt out of district surveys, marketing initiatives, and the like

In this final section, we return to the facts-and-find method to explore some of the complexities of two widely used federal acts that were amended by NCLB. These are the **Family Educational Rights and Privacy Act (FERPA),** 20 U.S.C. § 1232g, with regulations at 34 C.F.R. Part 99, and the **Protection of Pupil Rights Amendment (PPRA),** 20 U.S.C. § 1232h, with regulations at 34 C.F.R. Part 98. FERPA usually goes by that acronym or "the Buckley Amendment," after its original Senate author. PPRA is sometimes referred to by the names of authors of its several versions: "The Hatch Amendment," "The Grassley Amendment," or "The Tiahrt Amendment."

Facts

Public School security staff took witness statements and made reports to the police concerning an incident on school grounds. The reports were also provided to the school for student disciplinary proceedings. The district employs approximately 180 school security staff to monitor safety and security on its various school campuses. In addition to the security staff, the district has entered into a memorandum of understanding (MOU) with the local police department, which assigns police officers—referred to as Educational Facilities Officers (EFOs)—to specific schools in the district. The question presented is whether the statements and reports should be considered law enforcement records or whether they should be considered student **educational records** subject to FERPA.

Educational records protected information under the Family Educational Rights and Privacy Act, which public schools must make available for review by parents or eligible students and which cannot be released without their permission

With regard to records maintained by the district's security staff, in some incidents, the EFOs or other investigating police officers have taken the position that witness statements obtained by school security staff have been obtained for law enforcement purposes and should be made immediately available to law enforcement officers, as an exception to FERPA, especially in situations where a school incident involved behavior violating criminal law. The police department and other law enforcement agencies assert that they are entitled to access student statements and school security reports without obtaining a subpoena for these documents. The EFOs state that, in many situations, the investigative reports and witness statements secured by school security are prepared in furtherance of a law enforcement purpose and constitute the records of a law enforcement unit pursuant to 34 C.F.R. § 99.8.

The school district is concerned that school security staff, as school system employees, primarily support the administration and discipline of the schools and would not qualify as a separate law enforcement unit under FERPA. The investigations they conduct and witness statements they obtain are typically given to the school administration for use in student disciplinary matters.

Find

Both FERPA and PPRA are concerned with maintaining student privacy in districts receiving federal funds. FERPA requires districts to provide access to personally identifiable educational records to parents and "eligible students" (those 18 or over and those attending postsecondary institutions), giving them the right to correct and/or refuse dissemination to outside parties. There are exemptions, of course. The main exception to this rule is "directory information," defined in the statute as "the student's name, address, telephone listing, date and place of birth, major field of study, participation in officially recognized activities and sports, weight and height of members of athletic teams, dates of attendance, degrees and awards received, and the most recent previous educational agency or institution attended by the student" (20 U.S.C. § 1232g(a)(5)(A)). Another exemption, a controversial provision of NCLB, provides for distribution of student information to military recruiters unless parents or eligible students explicitly request nondisclosure.

FERPA defines educational records as "those records, files, documents, and other material which (i) contain information directly related to a student; and (ii) are maintained by an educational agency or institution or by a person acting for such agency or institution" (20 U.S.C. § 1232g(a)(4)(i) and (ii)). However, exempt from the definition are "records maintained by a law enforcement unit of the educational agency or institution that were created by that law enforcement unit for the purposes of law enforcement" (20 U.S.C. § 1232g(a)(4)(ii)). A minor, if notable, exemption was created by the Supreme Court in *Owasso Independent School District v. Falvo,* 534 U.S. 426 (2002), which held that peer-graded student work was not an "educational record," thus permitting this widespread practice to continue. In another FERPA ruling, *Gonzaga University v. Doe,* 536 U.S. 273 (2002), the Court held that a violation of FERPA does not entitle a parent or student to money damages, thus discouraging litigation by individuals in this area of education law.

PPRA provides for parental review of surveys, analyses, or evaluations of students in eight areas of protected subject matter, as well as distribution of student information for purposes of marketing or selling. The eight protected areas are:

1. political affiliations or beliefs of the student or the student's parent;
2. mental and psychological problems of the student or the student's family;
3. sex behavior or attitudes;

4. illegal, antisocial, self-incriminating, or demeaning behavior;
5. critical appraisals of other individuals with whom respondents have close family relationships;
6. legally recognized privileged or analogous relationships, such as those of lawyers, physicians, and ministers;
7. religious practices, affiliations, or beliefs of the student or student's parent; and
8. income (other than that required by law to determine eligibility for participation in a program or for receiving financial assistance under such program).

In addition, PPRA provides for parental rights to inspect, upon request, any instructional materials used as part of the curriculum and details the procedures for granting parental access.

In the complex and evolving environment of student privacy, educators must exercise caution. Whenever student information is transferred, educators should determine which law or laws apply and analyze each disclosure request in light of the applicable law. For example, if the disclosure request relates to an identifiable student's educational record, FERPA requirements should be researched. If the disclosure is for purposes of a survey, analysis, evaluation, or marketing, then the protected classifications under PPRA must be examined. Sometimes, questions can be resolved by applying the plain language of the statutes or regulations, or through reference to the district's FERPA/PPRA Notifications to Parents and Eligible Students. At other times, a quick phone call can be made to someone with student privacy expertise, such as a district specialist, professional association, or advocacy organization. Frequently, however, more complex analysis is required because novel fact situations often arise—school or student videos, for example—that require equally novel legal responses. In these situations, expert legal counsel is necessary.

The facts presented here clearly trigger analysis under FERPA and, in particular, its definition of personally identifiable "educational records" subject to parental (or nonminor student) inspection and permission before release. As stated, the question presented is whether the statements and reports should be considered exempt law enforcement records or whether they should be considered student education records subject to prior parent review and permission to release under FERPA.

According to a letter ruling concerning the Montgomery County, Maryland, School District, dated February 16, 2006, from the **Family Policy Compliance Office (FPCO)** that rules on FERPA and PPRA complaints, "FERPA no longer prevents a campus law enforcement division from disclosing to outside parties law enforcement unit records, including campus security incident reports, that were created by the law enforcement unit for a law enforcement purpose." Letter rulings are thus revealed as another important, though obscure, source of education law at the federal and state levels that invite the reader's further investigation.

Family Policy Compliance Office (FPCO)
the office in the U.S. Department of Education charged with determining Family Educational Records and Privacy Act and Protection of Pupil Rights Amendment enforcement issues

The letter ruling goes on to state—citing material published in the January 17, 1995, *Federal Register*, a daily federal publication that issues proposed and final regulations among other authoritative legal minutiae—that "[t]his does not prevent the District's security staff from also performing non-law enforcement unit functions such as administrative support and/or the disciplinary functions of the District."

The key, according to the letter ruling, is for the district to include its security unit and the police EFOs in its mandated annual notification to parents (34 C.F.R. § 99.7), announcing their dual roles as law enforcement personnel and as "school officials" (34 C.F.R. § 99.31) who, without prior parental review or permission, are permitted to share the material both with other law enforcement agencies and within the educational system, subject to the constraints of FERPA and any more rigorous state or local records access laws consistent with the federal statute. A

"Model Notification of Rights under FERPA for Elementary and Secondary Schools," as well as FPCO letter opinions and other FERPA and PPRA materials, are available on the U.S. Department of Education's website, www.ed.gov.

Glossary

30/60-day time line—the Individuals with Disabilities Education Act requirement that districts evaluate a student's educational needs within 30 days of referral and place the student in an appropriate setting within 60 days of referral

Adequate yearly progress (AYP)—the main standard of school and district progress under the No Child Left Behind Act

Americans with Disabilities Act (ADA)—statute requiring equal employment and physical accessibility for those with disabilities

***Carter* funding**—public financing of students in special education who have been placed in private schools by parents pending district determination of placement options

Education for All Handicapped Children Act (EAHCA)—the original federal law establishing educational rights for students with disabilities

Education of the Handicapped Act (EHA)—*see* P.L. 94–142

Educational records—protected information under the Family Educational Rights and Privacy Act, which public schools must make available for review by parents or eligible students and which cannot be released without their permission

Family Educational Rights and Privacy Act (FERPA)—the "Buckley Amendment," which provides privacy protections for identifiable student records

Family Policy Compliance Office (FPCO)—the office in the U.S. Department of Education charged with determining Family Educational Records and Privacy Act and Protection of Pupil Rights Amendment enforcement issues

Free and appropriate public education (FAPE)—the basic right of students with disabilities established by the Education for All Handicapped Children Act, Education of the Handicapped Act, and Individuals with Disabilities Education Act

Highly qualified teacher—the No Child Left Behind requirement that all students will be taught by certified teachers

Impartial hearing—a district-based proceeding initiated by a parent who disagrees with the school district's special education decision(s) concerning his or her child

Individualized educational program (IEP)—the required instructional plan for a child in special education to achieve learning objectives

Individuals with Disabilities Education Act (IDEA)—the current version of the federal law that requires public schools to make available to all eligible children with disabilities a free appropriate public education in the least restrictive environment appropriate to their individual needs

Least restrictive environment (LRE)—the precept that students in special education should be placed in the most mainstream instructional setting possible appropriate to their ability to learn

Limitations period—the time within which a legal action must be initiated

Local educational agency (LEA)—generally, a school district

Mainstreaming—placing students with disabilities with general education students

Manifestation determination review—a proceeding to ascertain whether the cause for disciplinary action arises from a student's handicapping condition, in which case such discipline is not permissible

Petitioner—the party initiating a civil action, particularly in an administrative proceeding (*see* respondent)

P.L. 94–142—the Education of the Handicapped Act, which established the modern set of substantive and procedural rights enabling students with disabilities to receive free and appropriate public education

Protection of Pupil Rights Amendment (PPRA)—often called the "Hatch Amendment," the law provides for student and parent access to review instructional materials and to opt out of district surveys, marketing initiatives, and the like

Related services—nonacademic interventions, such as occupational therapy and speech therapy, that permit students to gain from special education under the Individuals with Disabilities Education Act

Respondent—the party required to respond to a civil action, particularly in an administrative proceeding (*see* petitioner)

Safe harbor—under the accountability provisions of No Child Left Behind, states, school districts, and schools may still make adequate yearly progress if each subgroup that fails to reach its proficiency performance targets is reduced by 10 percent of the previous year's percentage if other targets are met

Scientifically based research (SBR)—the requirement under No Child Left Behind that instructional materials be validated as promoting student learning

Section 504 of the Rehabilitation Act—a federal statute barring discrimination against people with disabilities in federally funded programs

"Stay put" provision—the Individuals with Disabilities Education Act requirement that students in special education have a right to keep their current placement pending a final decision to change placement

Supplementary educational services (SES)—the right of students under No Child Left Behind to receive free tutoring and other after-school instruction if their schools fails to make adequate yearly progress two years in a row

Title I—the major federal education legislation targeted to assist low-income students but now subsumed within the broader mandates of No Child Left Behind

Unfunded mandate—the pejorative term for a federally required action by states and school districts without provision of sufficient federal funding to meet the requirements

References and Resources

The following references are cited in this volume.

The Constitution of the United States of America ("U.S. Constitution")

Article I, § 8, U.S. Constitution

Amendments 1–10, The Bill of Rights, U.S. Constitution

First Amendment, U.S. Constitution, Free Speech Clause

First Amendment, U.S. Constitution, Establishment Clause

First Amendment, U.S. Constitution, Free Exercise Clause

Fourth Amendment, U.S. Constitution

Eighth Amendment, U.S. Constitution

Fourteenth Amendment, U.S. Constitution, Due Process Clause

Fourteenth Amendment, U.S. Constitution, Equal Protection Clause

Statutes

20 U.S.C. § 1232g(a)(4)(i) and (ii)

20 U.S.C. § 1232g(a)(5)(A)

20 U.S.C. § 1412 (a)(10)(A)(i)(I)

29 U.S.C. § 706(8)(B)

Age Discrimination Act of 1975 and implementing regulations at 34 C.F.R. Part 110

Americans with Disabilities Act of 1990 (ADA), 42 U.S.C. § 12131 *et seq.*, and implementing regulations at 34 C.F.R. Part 35

Child Abuse Prevention and Treatment Act (CAPTA), 42 U.S.C. 5101, et seq.

Education of the Handicapped Act (EHA)

Equal Access Act, 20 U.S.C. §§ 4071–4074

Family Educational Records Privacy Act (FERPA), 20 U.S.C. § 1232g, and implementing regulations at 34 CFR Part 99 (Buckley Amendment)

Freedom of Information Act, 5 U.S.C. § 552

Handicapped Children's Protection Act (HCPA)

Individuals with Disabilities Education Act (IDEA)

No Child Left Behind Act

P.L. 94–142, Education for All Handicapped Children Act (EAHCA)

Protection of Pupil Rights Amendment (PPRA), 20 U.S.C. § 1232h, and implementing regulations at 34 CFR Part 98 (The Hatch Amendment, The Grassley Amendment, or The Tiahrt Amendment)

Section 504 of the Rehabilitation Act of 1973 (Section 504), as amended, 29 U.S.C. § 794, and implementing regulations at 34 C.F.R. Part 104

Student and Teacher Safety Act (proposed)

Title I, Elementary and Secondary Education Act (ESEA)

Title VI of the Civil Rights Act of 1964, 42 U.S.C § 2000d and implementing regulations at 34 C.F.R. Part 100

Title IX of the Education Amendments of 1972 and implementing regulations at 34 C.F.R. Part 106

Code of Virginia, § 22.1–279.1. Corporal punishment prohibited

Regulations, Regulatory Guidance, and Forms

Internal Revenue Form 1023

34 C.F.R. § 99.7

34 C.F.R. § 99.8

34 C.F.R. § 99.31

34 C.F.R. § 104.3(j)(2)(ii)

Connecticut Association of Boards of Education Formulation, Adoption, Amendment of Policies, 2004

Dubuque, Iowa Public Schools, School Board Policy Manual, § 1100, Curriculum Development, Implementation, and Evaluation (2001)

Guidance on Constitutionally Protected Prayer in Public Elementary an Secondary Schools, U.S. Department of Education, 2003

Los Angeles Unified School District, BUL-1347; Child Abuse Reporting Information Sheet; Administrator Certification Form 2006–2007, MEM-2558.1

Model Notification of Rights under FERPA for Elementary and Secondary Schools, U.S. Department of Education

New No Child Left Behind Flexibility: Highly Qualified Teachers, Fact Sheet, U.S. Department of Education, 2004

New York City Public Schools, Regulations of the Chancellor, A-412, A-432, D-160

Revised Sexual Harassment Guidance: Harassment of Students by School Employees, Other Students, or Third Parties, U.S. Department of Education, 2001, superceding prior Guidance issued in 1997

Students with Disabilities and Modified Achievement Standards, U.S. Department of Education Guidance, 2005

York, Maine Public Schools "Instructional and Library Materials Selection" policy and "Request for Reconsideration of Materials" (2002)

Judicial and Administrative Decisions

Association of Community Organizations for Reform Now (ACORN) v. New York City Department of Education, 269 F.Supp.2d 338 (S.D.N.Y. 2003)

Bethel v. Fraser, 478 U.S. 675 (1985)

Board of Education of Hendrick Hudson Central School District v. Rowley, 458 U.S. 176 (1982)

Board of Education, Island Trees Union Free School District No. 26 v. Pico, 457 U.S. 853 (1982)

Board of Regents v. Roth, 408 U.S. 564 (1972)

Brown v. Board of Education of Topeka, Kansas, 347 U.S. 483 (1954) (*Brown I*)

Davis v. Monroe County Board of Education, 526 U.S. 629 (1999)

Florence County School District Four v. Carter, 510 U.S. 7 (1993)

Garcetti v. Ceballos, 547 U.S. - (2006)

Gebser v. Lago Vista Independent School District, 524 U.S. 274 (1998)

Gonzaga University v. Doe, 536 U.S. 273 (2002)

Good News Club v. Milford Central School District, 533 U.S. 98 (2001)

Goss v. Lopez, 419 U.S. 595 (1975)

Hazelwood School District v. Kuhlmeier, 484 U.S. 258 (1988)

Honig, California Superintendent of Public Instruction v. Doe, 484 U.S. 305 (1988)

Ingraham v. Wright, 430 U.S. 651 (1977)

Irving Independent School District v. Tatro, 468 U.S. 883 (1984)

Keyishian v. Board of Regents, 385 U.S. 589 (1967)

Kitzmiller v. Dover Area School District, 400 F.Supp.2d 707 (M.D. Pa. 2005)

Lamb's Chapel v. Center Moriches, 508 U.S. 384 (1993)

Lemon v. Kurtzman, 403 U.S. 602 (1971)

Meredith v. Jefferson County Board of Education, 05–915 ((U.S. Supreme Court, 2007)

Meyer v. Nebraska, 262 U.S. 390 (1923)

Mitchell v. Helms, 530 U.S. 793 (2000)

Morse v. Frederick ("Bong Hits 4 Jesus"), 06-278 (U.S. Supreme Court, 2007)

Mozert v. Hawkins County Public Schools, 827 F.2d 1058 (6th Cir. 1987), cert. denied, 484 U.S. 1066 (1988)

Mt. Healthy City Board of Education v. Doyle, 429 U.S. 274 (1977)

Mueller v. Allen, 463 U.S. 388 (1983)

New Jersey v. TLO, 469 U.S. 809 (1984)

Owasso Independent School District v. Falvo, 534 U.S. 426 (2002)

Parents Involved in Community Schools v. Seattle School District, 05–908 (U.S. Supreme Court, 2007)

Pennsylvania Association for Retarded Children v. Commonwealth of Pennsylvania, 334 F.Supp. 1257 (E.D. Pa. 1971) (*PARC I*) and 343 F.Supp. 279 (E.D. Pa. 1972) (*PARC II*)

Perry v. Sindermann, 408 U.S. 593 (1972)

Pickering v. Board of Education, 391 U.S. 563 (1968)

Pierce v. Society of Sisters, 268 U.S. 510 (1925)

Santa Fe Independent School District v. Doe, 530 U.S. 290 (2000)

Smith v. Board of School Comm. of Mobile, 827 F.2d 684 (11th Cir. 1987)

Smith v. Robinson, 468 US 992 (1984)

Theno v. Tonganoxie Unified School Dist. No. 464, 377 F.Supp.2d 952 (D. Kan. 2005)

Tinker v. Des Moines Independent Community School District, 393 U.S. 503 (1969)

Virgil v. School Bd. Of Columbia County, 862 F.2d 1917 (11th Cir. 1989)

Zelman v. Simmons-Harris, 536 U.S. 639 (2002)

Zobrest v. Catalina Foothills School District, 509 U.S. 1 (1993)

Letter of Finding, Eden Prairie, Minn., Elementary School Sexual Harassment Incident, Chicago, Ill.: U.S. Department of Education, Office of Civil Rights—Region V (1993)

Letter Ruling concerning Montgomery County, Maryland School District, Family Policy Compliance Office (FPCO), February 16, 2006

Books, Periodical, Motion Picture and Websites

(in most cases, web addresses are preceded by "www.")

No Child Left Behind Primer by Frederick M. Hess and Michael J. Petrilli (New York: Peter Lang, 2007)

Questions Young People Ask—Answers That Work (Brooklyn, NY: Watch Tower Bible and Tract Society of Pennsylvania, undated)

Awake, periodical of the Watch Tower Bible and Tract Society of Pennsylvania

Bridges, J. (Director). (1973). The Paper Chase [Motion Picture]. United States: Twentieth Century Fox.

American Association of School Administrators
aasa.org

American Civil Liberties Union
aclu.org

American Federation of Teachers
aft.org

Center for Law and Education
cleweb.org

Cornell Law School Legal Information Institute (general legal information)
law.cornell.edu

Education Law Association
educationlaw.org

Findlaw (general legal information)
findlaw.com

Hieros Gamos (general legal information)
hg.org

Justia (U.S. Supreme Court Center)
justia.com

LexisNexis (general legal information)
lexisnexis.com

National Association of Elementary School Principals

naesp.org

National Association of Secondary School Principals
nassp.org

National Coalition for Parent Involvement in Education
ncpie.org

National Education Association
nea.org

National School Boards Association Council of School Attorneys
nsba.org/cosa

Oyez (U.S. Supreme Court media)
oyez.org

Parent Teacher Association
pta.org

United States Department of Education
ed.gov and 1–800-USA-LEARN

United States Family Policy Compliance Office
ed.gov/policy/gen/guid/fpco/index.html

United States Internal Revenue Service
irs.gov

United States Office for Civil Rights
ed.gov/about/offices/list/ocr/

Westlaw (general legal information)
westlaw.com